The Birthday Scrolls

Geoff Nicholls

First published in 2021
Published by Puncher and Wattmann
PO Box 279
Waratah NSW 2298
http://www.puncherandwattmann.com
puncherandwattmann@bigpond.com

NATIONAL
LIBRARY
OF AUSTRALIA

A catalogue entry for this book
is available from the National Library of Australia.

ISBN 9781922571113

Cover design by Miranda Douglas
Text design and typesetting by Morgan Arnett
Printed by Lightning Source

The Birthday Scrolls

21–60

Geoff Nicholls

PUNCHER & WATTMANN

Remembering Stuart Nicholls

Kenny had a dream

21   Leopard-Skin Pill-Box Hat

A package delivered from Armidale arrives at the upstairs door of Flat 2, *Eldnur*. It carries the dirt of social vacancy and a limited selection of clothes, is disdainful of shampoo, undernourished, and hopeful by rote. I am back, in the social order I had left, to acknowledge my twenty-first birthday in this solid rental block, away from an ear pricked to loneliness, for as long as they will have me. The residents rise to remember who I was.

We are in a lounge-room, overlooking Wolfe Street, that is state of the art for 1978. James weaves quickly translated patterns through everyone within reception. Don, informed by obscure insights, challenges others to feel the mirth that brushes his cheek. Vince, dangling like a spider juiced on cordial punk venom, runs across the backs of furniture before wrestling me to the floor. Davo stands starving quietly at the back door. Richard, famously proficient, heralds attention to being in harmony with his world by opening and closing a kitchen cupboard. I am not only entering this apartment, I am being drawn into it. Throughout, a live recording of Ian Dury and The Blockheads shouts about "Sex and Drugs and Rock and Roll!" James, who chose it, gives me a paraphrasing welcome, "Sex and drugs and English Literature, hey Nic?"

I take my place in our group, to descend Tyrrell Street like the shadows that play across its urban walls. We approach Civic Park and the Town Hall precinct in fighter plane formation, a band of bats seeking fruits on an evening in September.

We have the appearance of rebellious youth. Yet we mingle with the crowd congregating in the Civic Theatre's upstairs bar for tonight's screening of The Travelling Film Festival. I see myself here, amongst the theatre's orange and maroon inner walls and clean-clothed 'others', reflected on a wide mirror behind an upstairs bar. Because of my birthday, I am wearing this furry, second-hand, woman's church-hat called "the Rembrandt". Although I'm recognized by someone from high school, another self, standing self-consciously apart, looks out at her from inside his stoned world. A bat needing his cave.

A scene of dense European forest behind a sloping grass-land where a couple ride horses through the mist spreads serenely over the screen. Our shoulders, in a row, stand alert in the cinema's hushed darkness. My affront, at Vince's foolish chatter after the film's start, matures and unfolds as it reaches an intimate consciousness with Richard seated beside me.

Only a few words of recall are needed to project that dream-like forest again.

22   A Song from Under the Floorboards

She paddles, causing ripples on the bathwater's surface. An insignificant lapping along the tub's oval edge underscores her echoing, monotonic conversation. She has the voice of a detached sleepwalker. I press against the bath with reverence, loving Jean with a losing tonic that is both vigilant and vacuous.

She intones, "When Doncaster takes a bath... he asks me to play his slave."

I dutifully acknowledge that part of her life by imagining Don influencing her in that curious manner. My senses merge with the sickly paint and out-dated gas fittings in their satellite bathroom. For a moment, I re-experience the role of being a desperate trespasser.

Today, being my birthday, carries an added relevance. I dutifully offer this worth for auction, in episodes of a storyline that has, faintly, begun repeating.

Jean's bath has a spellbinding duration, drawing me to remain obedient to qualities constantly evading my grasp.

I stay. In honour of an invitation to her address on Corlette Street. Too aware that Jean and Don wrestle on a giant mattress over my head. I have asked, incomprehensibly, to share Jean's famously shaved pussy, offered at odd hours in my impoverished abode. But not here, where I risk being shot again, albeit benignly, on the floor of her cavernous bedroom. That there is no door there to help me be unseen, if I do.

"Could you get me the towel, Nic?"

She speaks in concert with driven splashes and streaming droplets as her naked body displays ascension. And I fetch it for her, seeing my birthright monogrammed in its tufted corner. But the dye is fading.

The swinging glass door opens at an angle. My initiating contact hinges on a negotiation of this acquiescent, yet poignant, impediment. Inside, I am met by an odour of stale plastic anchored on grimy metal, one peculiar to the interior of a phone booth. Enclosed in the intimacy, my nervous breathing couples with the halitosis of the telephone apparatus. Coins fumbled into a slot are followed by a pensive dialling. Each number is secured in an arc, until the sequence of 4-6-2-2-8-0 produces suspended binary tones culminating, gratefully, in an answering and a swallowing.

I have sought the voice of my family just as a goldfish gulps on flakes. A papery consciousness of origin, infused with an instinct for sustenance, flavours my being as I add words to those heard spoken from the home that houses the life I ceremoniously left.

In a corner of the fish tank, a phone booth in Cooks Hill, sanctuary settles listlessly, consumed by a hungry mouth.

23   Macarthur Park

Visitors to Hunter Hospital's Pryor House represent a distinctly different reality, their source is sunlit and vast. The patients here dwell in aimless currents of sea caves, and they shudder when normality intrudes. Their jealousy is soupy and indecent. While my family pours through a gap made by the open entrance doors, the neglected, sun-dried, bowling green seems to smirk from outside. Mum, Dad, Gemma and Rick combine to wish me well for my 23rd birthday. I try to bear their challenge against my loss of identity, but feel condemned by too much undermining medication. Too soon, their unconditional love is farewelled to endless light, while this 'voluntary client' is left behind at the threshold, supporting his cake instead.

"The cake that men like" is a family tradition defined by a generic dark fruitcake foundation sweetened under thick pavements of caramel icing. Nicholls' tongues are rumoured to have a predisposition toward its stock recipe, and our clan shares the dense flesh without query. In my present condition of hospitalisation with schizophrenia, however, this cake has more claim to a moniker than I do.

Some patients have formed links, navigating uncomplicated crafts close to mine, despite the stigma of mutual alienation. In this aquarium, housing mentally-ill odd-fish, any offer of a smokeable or edible treat attracts swift fins. A terrifying prospect of a feeding frenzy near to my braced heart and deflated genitals is, thankfully, allayed, as kindred swimmers gain only those slices a nurse cuts for them. Although, I must rescue the cake's bulk once other, graver, demands are observed.

Many of the roads in my madness have involved the transportation of a sacred item in need of protection. I roamed the extent of a lakeside park, seeking shelter among trees, while sinister beams investigated the secret cargo. Always, my loyalty was pledged to my secret's benevolent ruler. Today bears witness, either upstairs, on hallways leading to wards, or at empty locations in the grounds, to a talisman becoming cake-solid in the hands of its confused saviour. I am unable to return this special food to a society defined only by risk and indifference, so I keep it safe. Placed under garden shrubs where it will not be found.

24 Galleries of Pink Galahs

I attend these households because I am hungry, even stupid for company, and these are known abodes. I ascend the broad steps to a managerial verandah that overlooks New Lambton. My approach remains optimistic, although the disdainful, escaping air declares this residence to be another place of dead friendship.

Dave Burton entertains me inside with an intelligence that is undergoing the process of learning to avoid pity. His indifferent machinery makes provision for my foreign part because it assists his design's outcome. My hopefulness is practically encouraged. Dave dispenses hospitality from a production line, rolling pouch tobacco into cigarette papers then licking them sealed. Our conversation succeeds despite itself.

Dave's mother had loomed like a paranormal ogre over that time I stayed with his family as a guest. Then, he was a fatherless, growing teenager with posters of an elephant and a large blues woman dominating the bedroom wall. Maggie's lone-parent heaviness spread itself in a mode of mothering that was both vulgar and tender. The Burton brothers would sometimes exit through open windows in order to escape her pioneering hugs. Now, in homes of secondary occupation, they seek to disintegrate those sympathies that were aroused by primary care. Young men's talk cannot, however, completely resist the tug of raw tendencies. Having Maggie in common means that Dave and I can both love a little while smoking.

Sunburn usurps the surface of my nose. The scene of a back road sliced by drying creeks, and country-worn gum trees hosting galahs, somewhere between Bingara and Narrabri, floats beside my eyes and the spicy, red souvenir between them. I have also gained, from this recent wandering in early spring sunshine, the spirit of a parallel self who inhabits both his land and my 24-year-old skin. The younger Burton's and his housemates' ostracism insults me, yet I am reassured that, elsewhere, I stand accepted.

I visit another address, on Elizabeth Street in Tighes Hill. Here, to my satisfaction, I am recognised as someone with a pilgrim's aura. Don spreads a steaming pile of scallops and chips before us.

"Tuck in, Nic."

I join Don, Andy and Richard in a huddle over their food. We partake with goodwill, conscious that it is a birthday party meal. After eating, these friends, who are closer to me in age, surrender themselves to digestion. The evening, in dimming degrees, absorbs the room's three occupants until their shapes are strangely intangible.

I embark on a venture that leads me away, but to nowhere definite. A mythical exploration, walking alone at night-time, that has an easy governance. Local streets subside below averted roofs and under an unconscious sky. This is when loneliness conflates with naivety, when melancholy muzzles dangers, and risk resides only where its notification is bothered with. At such a liminal hour, the masked fangs of near traffic on Maitland Road are apprehended only due to random thoughts. I think I am about to jaywalk in front of the Tighes Hill Fire Station.

Other eyes are adjusted to this edge of reality, and they notice where a dreaming figure may require tactful orientation.

I hear Fay Russell's voice say again, "Hello Nic. Do you want a lift?"

She carries herself, upright and forthright, along the pavement as she approaches me. I'm really too silly to understand Fay's immediate concern. I register her genuine emotion because its illumination is significant in the muffled world around me. Her face, open and whole as an unmarked dinner plate, is positioned close enough to inspire trust.

I reply, "No thanks, but thanks for offering."

The man in shirtsleeves and loose trousers descends a wall into the broad storm-water drain. Distant streetlights delineate his crouched form as it makes its solitary passage beside the narrow, glimmering stain of sliding water. He stops to release a steady stream of urine that mixes jewels into the darkness. Then he straightens in self-congratulation.

25   Buffalo Soldier

Twenty-five-years-old today! And my appetite's whetted by the scent of savoury meat rolls escaping from the modest stove. Fatty lamb portions are wrapped, tongue-like, around embryos of seasoning and impaled on wooden skewers. Their vulgar postures bask in the oven's glow.

"Meat *rollies*! They're my favourite food!"

I turn to Gabriel who shares the narrow kitchen. His face breaks into a pleased smile that frees him from an undercurrent of solemn meditation.

"You said you liked them."

He speaks with a self-conscious Nigerian accent, in words weighted by deeper measurements.

We are sharing number nine Brien Street, The Junction. It is a small terrace, as empty as a used box. Our bodies inhabit more volume than any article of furniture does. Gabriel and I pass through this house like occasionally touching banners carried in on a prevailing wind. We are strangers as somebodies, but familiar because we are nobodies.

"Would you like to hear my song?"

I stand at his bedroom door looking in at the figure nursing a guitar. And he begins playing a gentle blues. Gabriel's yearning soul travels outward, singing above pitifully acute notes. I cannot let myself fall into that room. The acknowledgement I give him instead is to secretly escape. From the overgrown back garden, the welcoming front street, or in my dreams when I am asleep.

"This is unexpected!"

"Eat."

26 White Rabbit

Being progeny of Newcastle gains me righteous entry into the city's industrial parkland. The East-End foreshore houses railway sidings, also drawn from rightful character, that stand invitingly unfenced. Roving beings, such as mine tonight, are privileged to occupy them in this unattended scene.

My native form enters the holding yards under the night airs expired from Newcastle Harbour's suckling water. A wagon, left unclosed for those who belong to this stationary, doomed world, is my destination. I haul myself up into its firm interior and curl refugee-like on the carriage's floor.

My loneliness, beckoned by an inevitable calling, becomes a full sleep. It is a sleep of surrender, careless of the detecting probes that pass at intervals on a guard's torch-lit watch.

When a vivid morning light sighs on the incoming tide at the harbour-side of the track, my eyes open to a new day. This awakening conquers any prohibition that may have stalked my night-nurtured dreams.

The re-purposed HiAce van, affectionately known as "Neville Cush", arrives and Rick extends his hand in birthday greeting.

At the wheel of the transport vehicle, a carrier of idiosyncratic cargo, such as a boxed drum-kit, my brother maintains a hold that is lacking in his wayward older sibling. I sense this inferior worth, yet ride onward with an air of self-importance, both conscious that this is a familial act of favouring.

The Kartoon Kafé occupies a Sunday School room beneath Cooks Hill's Baptist Tabernacle Church. A short footpath descent on Dawson Street brings Rick and me to its frontage.

Michael Bell's artwork, featuring his iconic lettering, is strewn in a comical announcement over the conservative doorway.

Across town, traditions are undergoing a happy disruption due to the playful handling of local and current artists. Here, we enter their downstairs realm expecting to be tickled.

Our hostesses, ushering us to tables, are themselves participants in art. They skilfully negotiate the gaps between two-dimensional figures of Bell's trademark comics with a dutifulness that tends to overwhelm the setting.

On the table carefully painted miniatures of Pluto, Mickey, Minnie and Goofy titillate our fingertips from assembled crockery surfaces.

Michael takes a breath against his modesty to approach us. Noticeably embarrassed, but with customary earnest hospitality, he addresses me by my birth name.

"Thanks for coming Geoff... Pleased to meet you Rick... We've been getting a lot of interest... That's nice."

He gives a small wave, then offers complimentary cakes in acknowledgement of our patronage. Although their icings appear to be painted on, the tastes are real.

27 Diamond Dogs

I have no alternative than to discard the bicycle and run for cover under a tree. The magpie is extremely territorial. From behind the trunk, my bike looks stranded. This corner of Wickham Park belongs to that violent bird! It stares at me while gripping onto a naked, stuttering branch. I re-load some confidence. Shoulder pressed against bark, with challenged breath, I anxiously take aim before bounding ponderously toward my abandoned transport. At the same time, my foe conducts its next furious attack, scattering any composure I've found. Arcing in self-preservation, I jettison the bike's retrieval as the magpie completes another swoop. The trunk of a mature fig gives me a safe position to assess the probability of making an uphill rescue and escape. The bird also engages in a strategy between the trees. The fever of combat produces a harshly pitched charge.

"I have an appointment to keep, you bastard!"

My bike is re-gained with an offended cry. And then furious peddling.

Spike Milligan stands before us on the Civic Theatre's stage. Rick has arrived on time and we have found our row. Milligan's strange hair hangs in mop strands, his face, shaped by hilarity, appears transfixed in the spotlight. He proceeds to thwart paralysis with a torrent of words. Sadness retreats where Spike's humour succeeds. Our audience shares the warmth of his verbal blowtorch.

Rick and I part after the show with an exchange of the 1984 tour motto, "Strike while the iron is hot!"

For me, bicycling has become a process of discovery. This next day's morning ride reaches the smooth shell of Adamstown's velodrome. I marvel at the sight of a previously unknown arena.

Returning through Cooks Hill, two ladies in Queen Street arouse my passing interest. I have a curiosity about them that is tucked under my belly leaning forward for control. Their names, Meredith and Iris, are stored inside the safety helmet with fantasies. Cycling makes me hopeful.

Dressed again for the theatre and walking away from where I reluctantly board, I encounter a mate from schooldays. Ian Bale has a large head and bottom, a counter-balance of prominent apex and buttocks which prompted teasing in our childhood. The old taunt of 'Big-bum Bale-bird' sneaks across our afternoon reunion, but stays hushed.

Instead, Ian shares, "I've been involved in youth drama... This house is not my own... I'm starting another job with the bank."

I share, "I dropped out of university... I have no real direction... This is my birthday."

Today's meeting on Ian's Hamilton driveway suggests our common suburban past and schooling does mean something.

"Happy birthday Nic. And enjoy the play."

"Thanks Ian. Good luck with your job."

Then we step back into two lives hinging on a change of address.

I pass posters for Spike Milligan's last night show. Aunty Ruth, Dad, and Mum are waiting at the Civic Playhouse next door. Each gives me a birthday hug.

A comfortable neatness accompanies our filling of the designated seats.

Robin Ramsay, who performs tonight, has been resurrected from a fatal silo fall on *Bellbird* in 1967. Then, in a child's reaction to tragic television, I chanted, "Charlie's bit the dust!" Shamefully unaware that to my objecting mother the words danced too closely on her also-named father's grave.

Ramsay's Henry Lawson undoes his literary shirt, exposing raw complexions beneath. His smart city shoes are brushed with country dust. An Australian writer's hat is thrown into the breeze of generous applause for *The Bastard from the Bush*.

My folks and I gather afterwards for hot beverages in Kurt's Coffee Lounge. This building in Devonshire Street holds an archive of rendezvous stored in its tiered booths and smooth upholstery. We select from the seasoned hive's menu.

"Cappuccinos or hot chocolate?"

"Raisin toast?"

28   No, I Have No Regrets

"Hello brother, happy birthday... We are going well down here... looking forward to seeing you again. Look after yourself. Love you!"

Placing the handset back, a sense of belonging infuses the house where I am considered different.

A rental arrangement is by default an experiment. Games are played that may be pledges of fellowship or statements for departure because of their rules. We "pass the caviar around", "have aches and pains", and "keep hobbies alive", as people should. Only, our interests, too often, seem to take divergent paths.

"Don't you have a key?"

"Yes. I just thought it easier to knock."

So my face grows longer until a stranger on a Merewether bus notices.

"Comme ci, comme ça."

Then I know my days here in Selwyn Street are numbered.

Gemma's call was generous for an STD from Canberra. During its length my attention has transferred from an empty carpet over to a curtain now touched with light. The material lifts just enough for meaning to enter. And for the time on the wall to remind me that I am late for school.

Tighes Hill TAFE stands, bricked and proud, to meet the students who enter her campus from parklands under trees, and off car parks that shoulder concrete drains.

A roomful of characters, conscientiously gathered for An Introduction to Welfare, surrounds me. There's Ronald, who finds salvation through pressing a musical reed to his moustached lips. Big Reg, who fights on the inside while the world outside throws punches on his shoulder, whose hands are buried deep and wrap themselves around the reins of a wild horse. One day they doused him in honey to quell all those stinging bees, "Today is the date I was converted to Christianity." Olive may have had a nervous breakdown. Sheila is always fidgety. Gay Paul remains constantly earnest and nice. Loud Bertha expounds from a platform of cosmetics and fashion. Together, we are students of the 'caring profession'. Individually, we are proof of its relevance.

Eventually, I make a departure from our tertiary education. My walk carries me under a stately row of Moreton Bay figs alongside Islington's Maitland Road in an easterly direction to Newcastle.

Allan receives me at the entrance to his ground floor flat off Parnell Place. His studious mind is rolling with anticipation. It is evident that he hopes to make an occasion of tonight's visit. In the past, we have shared exhilarations. Under a.m. streetlights, our late-night foraging uncovered treasures worth of piled snapshots, seconds found in garbage bins outside photo-labs, which we later scrutinised, with a pirating thrill, on his bare floor. Yet, we have also endured the difficulties of a mutual trust that has been cautioned by too many violations. To enter Allan's world means we must both risk suspicion. This time, however, he makes a proposal we can each accept.

"Let's go for a walk, Nic. I want to show you something."

We follow the hedges of the harbour's foreshore, gradually flattening into contours along the port. His surprise for me becomes apparent. Triangles of red light, usually acknowledged with indifference as functions of an unknown signage, have simultaneously aligned themselves over extended intervals to create a single navigational beacon. Only travellers on broad waters, such as sea mates on a common journey, could make this special discovery.

We return, like fellow pilgrims with maps in our heads, to the greeting servery of Jerry's Fish Café. The proprietor, with a gunning English accent, addresses our custom while reaching, sonorously, over crescendos of frying food. Our mouths soon fill with the fluffy tang of takeaway fish cakes. We eat never too far from a garbage bin so to toss inside the oily, leftover white paper bags.

Assisted by the first hands of daylight, and heavy with sleeplessness and indigestion, I mount the windowsill of last night's uninhabited Selwyn Street bedroom. My conscience appears to be waiting for me in the neglected manchester of its peaceful annex. A wrapped present and card from my housemates are placed on the empty bed.

"But I didn't think my birthday would have mattered to you."

"We think birthdays are special times, too."

And I remember the soothsayer's French on a bus that did not set down passengers for Merewether.

"Comme ci, comme ça."

"*So, so.*"

And I know my days here are numbered.

29 You Are My Sunshine

The arrival of spring is like a blessing, its soaking sunshine coincides with my birth date. The Peace Banner Project team joins me on a break to share today's promising warmth.

Weathered deck planks on the verandah act as seats. Faded pastel exterior walls form wings facing the courtyards they enclose. I sit in meditation, work-tired and surrendering to the nurturing bustle of grass leaves as they photosynthesise. To my left, a Community Arts Centre tap holds court over the basin of a ceramic drain. The weeks in cavernous class-rooms producing thematic banners for 1986's Year of Peace have seen daily paint-caked tubs and brushes washed under outpourings of water from that brass head. Each of us has converted to the cause of depicting peace. As the vigour of youth. In a threatened natural environment. With hands of religious culture merged in a single pattern. Or doomed by the mushroom cloud. And championed with the flags of nations. Our creations have become statements that are tacked to dry slowly on the walls where we toil. I feel blessed, and savour their achievement.

Gitte emerges from one of the studio doorways, her presence preceding her physical form. She looks like the supervising artist. An adhering intent gives her face a look of Scandinavian masculinity. Wiped and smeared colours stick to an over-sized t-shirt serving as a smock. Tracksuit pants grip around the ankles of her bare feet. She has led us into artistic battle singing the hymn of the Golden Section. We have marched with a soldierly loyalty behind the smoke from Gitte's Alpine cigarettes. They have instructed us in research and selection, outlining and completion. We have employed an instrument standing before each banner, aimed like a gun-placement, which projects images from weighty books and sorted magazines.

"Follow me... because I follow you."

The summoning of her Danish-Australian accent prompts us to end our paddle in this sunshine's delightful respite.

Today's guest speaker is a doctor from Newcastle's Hunter Hospital. She addresses us with professional confidence in a deliberate manner that expounds without giving extraneous information. Either due to an embodiment of mental health's 'tough love', or in her objective delivery of the institution's themes, our speaker's presentation affects us with its nobility of cause.

Doctor Attika's tall, weather-beaten figure wins respect from her listeners, who also function dutifully. An aspect of the banner project has been to expose us to those organisations concerned about the welfare needs of the marginalised. We have begun to hear a certain heartbeat emanating from places where guardian angels and creative rights are found.

I am aware of Gitte standing behind our forward-facing chairs, guiding us with her intellect, intuition, and compassionate veins. I would like to question Doctor Attika about the psychiatric hospital's saturating use of medication, or what has become of her colleague, Doctor Wazoo, who had drugged patients dance in callisthenic circles, but these enquiries subside along with my lame memories. Besides, this afternoon's visitor has a dignity that makes an irrelevance of someone who would have crawled, ignored, in halls outside offices like hers.

"I'm having my birthday today," I confess to Lou Beyer's lingering interest.

Lou's presence is dexterous, she shares her studies at university with the banners, and shares her attention between me and her reserved self. I figure that her methodical sensibility derives from her German background. She responds without celebrating my status too much.

"Today? That's interesting."

Nightfall brings a less neutralised light that shines brightly from a small bulb. This gift of a bicycle lamp was Rick's idea. The Cat-Eye is made in Germany. I explore its moulded black casing. The battery compartment is clasped with a prominent screw. It can be secured to the handlebar using an attached, tightened belt. The ribbed switch is easily engaged with a thumb movement, then portions of flat darkness become highlighted under a probing beam.

30   Let's Go Fly a Kite

Mum and Dad occupy the farmhouse's front verandah. They convey a keen interest in what I am doing. It is as if their child is unwrapping a present from a time when being a family was simply romantic. Although my maturity may be compromised by such attention, I adhere to the unconditional generosity it presents.

Dad asks, with an unforced geniality in his voice, "Does it fit?"

"It's great, Dad. Thanks very much to the both of you."

Then, leaving the newly fastened bike rack, I exhibit my gratitude by giving each of my parents a muscular, and softly received, hug. A great space becomes intimate with affection given. Blue crops of mountains beyond us form a horizon before which stationary tree armies line at edges of gently rising paddocks reaching, in turn onto the friendly mown lawn that serves this scene of bicycle maintenance and special family history.

I return from the superficiality and timelessness of maternal and paternal embrace to my bike, as some nuts still need tightening toward an inevitable acclaim.

"How does it look?"

I hold the bicycle upright, with the useful rack extending over its back wheel.

"Like a bought one!" Mum declares.

"But it is a bought one, dear," Dad reminds her.

We have driven into Newcastle from Quorrobolong during the morning. Compared to the previous day's rural repose, the atmosphere inside Rick's shared house on Gordon Avenue has me drawing a complex breath. My brother hands me an album enclosed in a plastic dust jacket. The Pogues' *Rum, Sodomy & The Lash* is a purchase made thanks to a prior consultation. I relish the cover's cheeky depiction of an Old Master's painting of an orgy of sailors clinging to a tilting raft, their heads comically usurped by those of the Irish folk-punkers.

"It's my thirtieth birthday and I got a bicycle rack!"

But whatever humour I intended only increases my self-consciousness in front of Rick's late-rising friends.

Somewhere along the road down to Campbelltown, probably after a rest stop, I remind Rick to fasten his seatbelt.

"Rick, you have to have your seatbelt on when the car is in motion. Could you please fasten your seatbelt?"

"Do you have to sound so morbid about it?"

A sudden shaft of hate drives through my brother and me, as intense as if the car has had a collision. Strapped down and in constant momentum, our emotions begin to fester, like the stale air trapped inside the automobile. Thoughts of words to solve this mounting and puzzling tension are savoured, then swallowed, like the patches of scenery periodically sustained outside the window. Most challenging is the impulse to cross the division of violence and to embrace Rick over his restraint.

Dad parks the car in a downtown Campbelltown road adjacent to a park that I recognise from a previous visit. Some locations don't change as much as others, thus linking their identities more closely to memory.

After strolling, in our family's fashion, around the nearest shopping centre, we return, with the heat of a takeaway pizza warming through its cardboard, to that earlier site.

Rick and I are seated beside each other in the back of the car. The mercury of our sullen feud is still, boldly and banally, high. The family-sized pizza, placed between us, expels pungent odours in dull prompts about confused goodness. Our tempers, by degrees, decrease, while our transport finds a way to Aunty Ruth's new home in Bradbury. I dread the moral imperative of arriving at her uncorrupted door.

The table is laid for us and the pizza is officially liberated from the confines of its box and served. Each warm division acts as an inclusive gesture, both of reunion and celebration of a birthday. But I cannot love the food, nor can I be loved by my family's company.

"I'm sorry, but I don't feel like eating pizza. I think I'll go for a walk now."

All eyes and hearts around the table sink. Aunty Ruth, by making local street directions known to me, nurses my melancholy bid. Her affectionate help is as sure a guarantee as I can hope to get.

When I wander, '... *lonely as a cloud*,' Bradbury's alien causeways, some sense of escape filters from their guilty culverts. However, only the emptiness of that scenery accompanies my sheepish knock an hour later on Aunty Ruth's front door. Whatever resilience I carry back to Mum, Dad and Rick in the lounge-room seems wasted fortitude, because it is used to withhold one meaningful brother's hug from their upraised hearts and eyes. I retire early upstairs, onto the neatly made bed in the tidy, spare bedroom.

Just as breakfast and kindred farewells fill my last night's hunger, so the fact that we have left to travel further south allows for a return to direction. I am a passenger re-emerged with his family, urged onwards by the Hume Highway passing rhythmically beneath Dad's steering, Mum's navigation, and Rick's silence.

Somewhere in the mountains outside Canberra, a stiff wind lifts a multi-coloured box kite on its inaugural flight. As it arcs and flutters at the end of an unravelling string, Gemma and Arlo's present carries with it a transcendent hope. Released by the abandoned run that launched it, I feel younger, and part of an action which brings us together on this sloping picnic ground. Rick, with a cigarette snared between his hirsute lips, joins in the applause which accompanies my kite's becoming airborne. Smiles tighten a little, though, when the plastic bird dives recklessly on a gust to perch, beyond reach, in the branches of a grand tree that has probably seen this type of landing before.

31   Sweet Surrender

Mornings in this subterranean bedroom have an autonomous life. After sleep has taken me away, folksy dancers weave an awakening into a common rousing. When my eyes open, the measurement I make, in seeing the distance that lies between the broad mattress on the floor and the pale blue wall, is the day's first act. Reality, like a sickness, arrives soon after. And, the dancers, in retreat, depart beneath a skirting board.

An actual dawn has passed to be replaced by another, second, dawning. Normality requires conforming to their dual reasoning. The one, earlier, is carried by the sun, and compels awareness to rise, and the other, later, adjusts variousness to a single, determined, repetition.

On some days, just getting out of bed can happen on the *wrong side*. I stagger up, in a yawning state and barefoot, onto bed linen and then on stained timber flooring. I make my way out, out of mind, and out of sorts. It is an irritable beginning to my 31st birthday.

From where I sit, on the breakfast step of flat 5/8 McCormack Street, lunch does not seem too far away. I notice how expansive the sunlight is. It catches on the clustered leaves and the dilapidated fences, and on the stairs that shield my door from city bustle.

In ascending the side path to the one-way street, I am aware of the poetry in familiar routes being inseparable from the progress of the soul. These images of a low brick wall, cracked concrete, and weeds in lasting grey light, are a part of me. I pass low-slung verandahs, three in a row, before

I take the steep descent down the metal railings in Church Walk Park.

A voluminous air impresses itself against my dreamer's limbs, striding on to a rendezvous on Hunter Street.

Keith is on his lunch-break from Telecom, Rick between shifts at the BHP. The three of us huddle around a low table, acquainted equally with the sun shining under the front door and with the Clarendon's front bar. We each have schnitzels, chips and salad on our plate. Schooners of Tooheys New stand affixed in liquid amber in the natural light. The cutlery also has a subdued glint. Our attention is on the drink and food, which we swallow with carnivorous, yet not unkind, gestures.

"Well Geoff, I have to get back to work."

"Yeah brother, I've got an afternoon shift to get to."

I sit at the table after they have left, acknowledging today's resolute air embracing me once again.

An alcoholic light-headedness probably explains the level of contentment that I get from the twelve-year-old Rank Arena's purplish screen. I sprawl back on the red upholstery of the car seat that serves as a lounge in my flat, to watch *How Green Was My Valley?* on Channel Three. Hedges, stone walls, coalmine mouths, miners' lamps, and stern expressions on dirty faces in humble kitchens, all appear as the Welsh story unfolds, painfully and sentimentally, in black and white.

When I venture outside, I notice how beautiful weather has fallen upon our derelict backyard, and my inferior existence. And it shames me that my distemper from this morning's out of sorts shuns the ideal that is offering its bosom here.

The novelty of the Stable Table, its light density between my hands and nursed on my lap, occupies me inside for a while longer. The tray's useful portability is already established, as Mum and Dad have had theirs for years. Giving this one to me as a gift maintains a family practice of sharing signature goods. The object of my balance now represents both an inheritance and an heir. However, the lack of trust in providence that undermines the day causes me to set the table down, unadopted in a quiet corner, while I pursue a real outcome instead. This afternoon prefers an amoral destiny.

After the generic doorbell has played an empty echo, the hostess appears to give a friendly welcome. Each time I pass into the Body Care Centre on King Street, a quality of cheap anticipation enters too. Amy greets me as a regular, then she leads me for the short distance down the hall to our room, where she leaves me temporarily alone. With a controlled urgency, I undress, re-acquainting myself with the posters of women in skimpy gym outfits, in stereotypical poses, and of massage zones, illustrated fore and aft, with the clean towels draped along the clothes-rack, and with my bearded nakedness mirrored back.

While I support my forehead on the padding, at the head of the massage table, my face protrudes through an opening, and onto a view of carpet.

Amy returns, and closes the door behind her. Her oiled hands proceed, with considered manipulation, from my stubborn heels, up my muscular calves and thighs, until they reach a swollen junction and culminate in conspiratorial tickles. She must be aware of an explosive need responding to this touch, as she prompts me to roll over for a hand-relief, its gushing release, coming after her strokes, cleaned by dexterous wipes from a nearby box of tissues. She smiles knowingly, she has the grounded sensibility of a tradesperson at work.

"Turn over and I'll finish your back."

I do so, conscious of a primal weight dislodging in my body. My back, my shoulders, my neck, succumbing to her symmetrical kneading.

"Turn over."

And over I go. Amy's massage directs the flow of my being. Like a lesson going to an inevitable ending, it instructs me to come once, then twice, to where I learn to no longer count the times!

"You are an expert."

"Happy birthday."

And she gives a special kiss to my lips.

I have, at last, found the ninth of September. This time, all of me dismounts from the *right side* of the bed.

32 Green Door

"Hello my name is Geoff. I am collecting for the Freedom from Hunger Annual Doorknock Appeal. Would you like to make a donation?"

"Hello, I am Geoff. I'm collecting for the Annual Doorknock Appeal for Freedom from Hunger. Would you like to make a donation at all? Any amount would be gratefully appreciated."

Hello. Do you doorknock? I'm Geoff. My name is Freedom from Hunger. How would you like to appeal?

A game develops in my thoughts, to counteract the repetition. I left McCormack Street this afternoon to continue a charity drive. It has taken me over the streets that form the residential crest of Newcastle's Hill area. Many polite pounds and doorbell pressings, followed by doormat waits for occupants who reveal themselves with various modes of welcome, has led me to arrive at this useful distortion.

Each dweller has passed across either their stamp of uniqueness or their currency, or both. I have given handwritten details on receipts and a personal statement of gratitude in exchange. The weighted cash bag is moulding to my side. Although inhaling the freshness of these encounters, my being has gradually sunk like an expiring lung.

Knock. Knock. Knock.

Knock and knock and... knock.

And.

"Hello, my name is Geoff. Would you like to donate to the Freedom from Hunger Annual Doorknock Appeal?"

"Yeah, sure, I'll just find my wallet."

He goes inside a neatly furnished apartment. A weekend ambience softly emanates from within. When he returns,

I notice he is a well-groomed, solid gentleman, casually dressed, perhaps a man who may require extra assertion to overcome his self-doubt.

"Will five dollars be enough?" he enquires.

"Yes, that will be great. Thank you very much," I reply.

I think out aloud, as I attend to writing the date on his receipt, "The ninth of September... it's my birthday today."

"It's mine too," he declares with surprise, then looks towards me with a curiosity that I cannot relate to.

What is shared and what is unshared evokes a paradox. We make a transaction of goodwill. But it sounds peculiar expressed in this unfamiliar hallway.

The bohemian grandeur of Jesmond House suits me better. I enter her cobbled courtyard with the zeal of a traveller arriving from a long journey. There is a residence at ground level I have visited before.

Catherine O'Malley had, within days of departing for Europe, invited me into her place there. Small pictures and intensely written words were posted on various surfaces. Something was making her tremble about my presence. Her departure was not so important to me, yet an emphatic requirement that I should understand more sank into my heart.

Another tenant answers the pensive, wilful intrusion of those ground-floor memories.

"Ja? How can I help you?"

Catherine's spirit seems to flicker beyond this handsome German accent.

The good health of the present occupant reclaims a sense of purpose that was lacking in my visit four years ago.

A beautiful, olive-skinned lady appears at his side. I am swept clean of thoughts. She is a singer and her mentioning of a gig in Cooks Hill tonight feeds the hunger of this determined collector.

With a revitalised spiel, I meet another resident on a verandah overlooking the courtyard. He represents the last appeal in Jesmond House, the grand old building that once lodged Samuel Clemens.

I cross Barker Street from fame to fame as Olivia Newton-John's family home beckons from that corner. Nobody answers its blue door in a brick wall.

It is heartening when an engaging, familiar person does open for me. Colin Day's wide-awake eyes invite me into the downstairs passage of one of those terrace houses that stand, buck-toothed, between more recent constructions. I follow his chirping voice up the padded, carpeted, stairs.

"Sam. We've got a visitor," he announces to his wife.

Hello. My name is Geoff. I am collecting... I stop myself from reverting to the hackneyed spiel, and say something cordial to her.

We had previously crossed windy paths in a rambling art school house on Laman Street. Her flirtatious nature had humbled me then. Now she has elegance, ornamented by her vivid ginger hair and dress with an emerald and white floral design.

"Of course I remember you. It's good to see you again, Geoff."

Husband and wife then join to enact an eager account of yesterday's robbery.

"We were at home at the time."

"My wallet had 200 dollars in it."

"We used to leave the front door unlocked."

"The thief must have known we were inside."

Their disbelief is contagious. I am shown the counter on the upstairs landing from where the money was stolen. The closed front door below appears to be keeping a secret from us.

Sam pours glasses of Colin's home-brewed beer, taken from a bottle kept stoppered in the fridge. He offers me a stained timber chair to sit in. I acknowledge their toast and the intoxicating taste of the alcohol.

My following conversation spills into the room like a mercifully pierced swelling. They did not know that a successful mutual acquaintance once dallied with heroin. We presume his marriage and political career mean that he would not risk himself again. Colin and Sam are bemused by my (almost boastful) revelation.

When I declare my intention to see a band tonight, Colin remarks that they no longer go out because it is a scene they have outgrown. A sneaking recollected moment, when randy and boozed, intrudes on my perception of the mature relationship nestled comfortably before me. To say, "that's because you don't need to", occurs as an unsuitable statement of fact, so I let the obvious comment drop.

Sam and Colin want to accompany me on my walk home. The three of us embark, after locking up, onto the street, where our discussion seeks ownership over any lurking mischief. I adjust to their stride with an afternoon's collected money nudging unselfconsciously against my chaperoned hip. We weave our way along intersecting climbs onto Tyrrell Street and descents into Church, until reaching the walled one-way block where I live.

Samantha gives me a clean, tight, birthday hug just outside number five's green door. I carry its sensation inside like a temporary famousness.

Hello, my name's Geoff... "A schooner of New, please."

"Two–eighty?"

Thanking the barmaid, I draw back from the beer-mats, as other drink orders are pending.

A cavity against The Oriental's Bull Street wall allows me to view the group on stage. Their gangster trombone player is giving emphasis to a Latin brass pronouncement. I know his mug-shot bravado from other bands. A jumble of funk sends the crowd into another trance or a dance.

During an interlude, I take respite in the small, adjacent poolroom. The fellow from Jesmond House is without his vivacious South American wife.

"Hallo. The band is very good, eh?"

"Yeah. It's just my style of music."

"Can I get you a beer?"

Well, it *is* my birthday. "Okay... thank you. I'll still be here."

Dieter returns with two green-labelled stubbies of Victoria Bitter.

I make a point of shaking Dieter's hand in farewell before leaving during the next set.

For a disappointed moment, I orientate myself outside the hotel, then commence the solitary walk back home.

My name is Geoff.

Sometimes there is no following address to canvass.

I am collecting.

And no better luck to be found.

Will you donate?

33   Back in Black

Rick's voice calls respectfully to announce their arrival. His brotherly profile appears downcast, framed briefly in the small viewing window. I open up to welcome the couple back. Each supports a bowl of prepared food. Five months away has given them a worldly look. Rhonda stands beside the man she will marry, following his movements like an extension of his clothing.

Rick occupies my kitchen to heat our meal. Images of an inebriate towing a cart, and a toucan juggling a pint on its beak, are stuck above the counter next to where he keeps busy. Ten Guinness Stout twist-tops that dad has donated sit in the cupboard without a door and complement Rick's postcards from Dublin.

I am shown the photographs that weren't stolen from their van. They spent three weeks in Edinburgh fitting it out for travel. Rhonda says they named it Hank because the only tape they had was Hank Williams' songs. I notice the level of skill evident in Rick's renovations, of making panels and cupboards to suit their needs. The photos sit in piles on the Stable Table placed between us.

Stories about Romania depict a nation with an impoverished society. On one occasion, Rick and Rhonda parked beside an apparently deserted road into a town. However, when they began eating, children appeared from nowhere and were clinging to their clothes begging to be given something! Of all the countries in Europe they saw, they exclaim in unison, it was Romania that gave them the worst impression.

Berlin had plenty of cafes open at night. Many visitors arrived at the site of the demolished Berlin Wall. Vendors were selling pieces of it. The fragment of chipped concrete, stained by a red streak of paint, which I hold, is one. I make the comment that I now have two souvenirs from Germany, a moulded rubber clamp found at the construction site of the Munich Olympics and this symbolic gift in 1990.

They leave while daylight still sends its downward spell through the trees.

The ten bottles of stout remain unopened. An unusual amount, they should last for a while.

34　Message in a Bottle

I arrive home from the Shortland Wetlands on this Friday afternoon. As the day's effort relaxes itself at the familiar green door, I spy a piece of folded paper wedged underneath.

DEAR GEOFF. "It's a girl" 7 ½ lb's. 22 ½ inches. You beauty!!! Rick.

It's good news... Yet I'm without a phone and with the coming weekend at work... They'll have each other and the grandparents, though... I bet Rhonda is stuffed!

Rick's handwriting appears to wriggle with excitement.

I savour my brother's note as a keepsake.

I am performing the job of a marshal for this Sunday's "Ironbark Creek Canoe Challenge". Teams assemble to take their turns. Eleven-foot-long orange Wobbegong canoes are aligned and waiting for them on the launching ramp. The interference of wake and bubbles from the previous competitor's start dispel just as another group embarks on the watery plane. Residual curls of stripped orange plastic left behind remind me that the eroded bitumen slope into the trail needs replacing. I pay attention to the next challenger's name, The Spinsters, and their time of departure, 11 am. When they return, I check their muddied answer sheet, twenty out of twenty, and time taken to visit the listed locations, one hour and eight minutes.

Gerard arrives at the canoe shed on his yellow Apollo racing bike. My friend is over six feet tall, so his appearance crossing the grounds occupies the centre of my attention. He and I have been keeping company since we met through

Amnesty International and found that we lived quite near each other. I've thought of us as a Mutt and Jeff combination, or any other characterisation of mates sharing a notable difference in height. The University of Newcastle has its Open Day and Gerard, in his role as a senior lecturer, has been hosting laboratory tests. I am surprised at the size and thoughtfulness exhibited by the extra-large t-shirt he presents to me.

"Happy birthday for tomorrow, Geoff. Something to remember Open Day with!"

I have immersed myself, on this Monday off, in an education which has morphed into a quest against an insidious monster's invasion. An *Ag-Fact* titled "Alligator Weed" contains recent information on noxious aquatic vegetation. Adaptable propagules occupy the study desk. Hand-drawn, labelled pictures of *Alternanthera philoxeroides* come with dire warnings. Their neat illustrations wrestle to control a mythical, amphibious army. Prolonged concentration tends to produce this exaggerated effect. I concern myself with its existence in preparation for tonight's presentation to my horticultural botany class.

I take the 322 bus to tech at Kahibah, carrying my report sorted into a folder in a large shoulder bag and charged with a story to tell!

The appeasing expression of our scholarly substitute teacher advises us, "It is probably best to postpone the class talks until next week's lesson when Henry is back."

I am consoled that disaster in our waterways and farmlands has, on this occasion, been diverted.

"I guess I live to fight another day," I say to Pete, who gives me a lift back into town.

He smiles, and replies in his mellow, suave British accent, "Yes, I guess you do!"

Pete Davidson's profession as a psychiatrist must lead to a consultation manner that sets people at ease.

He drops me at the mailboxes on McCormack Street.

"Good night."

He drives his unloaded car around the corner and a few blocks up Church Street to where he and his artistic spouse, Bubba, live.

A figure, segmented by filtered nocturnal lighting, stands before the downstairs entrance to number five. He is instantly recognisable.

"Rick! I've been looking forward to seeing you!"

"Happy birthday, brother."

Our words intermingle with our embrace.

"Congratulations on becoming a father!"

"So you got my note?"

"Yeah, I've put it with the treasures."

"We've decided to call her Kerry Rose. A bit confusing for the in-laws with us having a last-minute name change, but Rhonda and I have agreed on this one. She's a beautiful thing. It amazes me that something that wonderful came out of my dick," he giddily explains.

My hand shakes his.

"How's Rhonda?"

"She's doing surprisingly well. She had to be pretty drugged-up during the birth. She's just tired now, they came home from hospital on Sunday. Oh, she said to wish you happy birthday."

"Thanks, Rhonda."

"So, Geoff. Do you mind being Kerry's godfather?"

"Not at all, I'd be honoured."

"Good. There's nobody else to ask with Rhonda not having any brothers or sisters."

"Yeah... "

"Well, will we see you tomorrow to meet our new girl?"

"You bet. Good on you mate. Give my love to Rhonda... and Kerry Rose!"

My brother's figure departs up the side path with a flurry of a waving hand, his cheerful grin is captured in a shaft of street light.

35   Messenger Boy

Sam Shepard's appearance on the screen is of a middle-aged man wearing suits that give him, in the film's scenes, an outdated look. The present setting of *The Voyager* is in the 1950s, however his character's lack of fashion is only an accessory to the man's disembodiment from contemporary time. He represents a mode of existence that falls into a space outside the occurrence of events. Shepard's "Harry", I think, is an engineer by profession and in outlook. His eyes reside behind wide spectacle frames, making them look lost in unresolved computations about life.

The women of the story are in turns poetic, youthful, mature, and urbane. They dash their lives against Harry's restless chest as waves attempt to embrace the station of a rock.

Every portrait of modern man that has occupied my record covers, music videos, and dust-jacket photos, meets in the displaced demeanour projected before me in this nearly empty cinema. I depart the venue with a handsome traveller's identity, and broker my way through Hunter Street's mid-afternoon, mid-week population.

This evening's clientele at the Cambridge Hotel are, by comparison, less numbered. Rick and I obtain our beers from a front bar setting that resembles the interior of a Viennese café. Patrons' backs maintain disinterested postures while we take our foaming schooners into the rear room. We have the curvature and nightclub mural of the venue area to ourselves. Once we are seated at one of the podium tables, Rick presents me with a colourfully covered paperback. Its title reads, *The Mambo Kings Play Songs of Love*. His well-read wife, Rhonda, has again made a sharp choice of book. I receive their gift with anticipation, as the prospect of a story that combines immigrant life in New York with the exotica of Cuban music is a vivid lure to my inner swagger. It prompts me to recollect, "I was here last Tuesday night to see The Human Beings play in the front bar."

"Is that Mark Johnson's band? He plays the flute?"

"Yeah, he leads the band... a bit different having a flute up front. They're a good combination, double bass, cello, electric guitar and Nic Cecire on drums, mellow and jazzy. They remind me of Frank Zappa."

"Wouldn't mind playing jazz myself. I've been having good jams with Chris and Steve Evans, really heavy, grungy stuff... like Wire. You'd like it."

"I remember when you used to play along to Wire downstairs at Eleebana. It drove Mr McAllister up the wall!"

My memory of a younger Rick ensconced behind his drumkit matches with the controlled energy of the brother perched before me and offering to get me another beer. He drinks at a greater rate than I do, but I accept for my birthday's sake.

While Rick is gone, I contemplate the flickering options of a newer version of a jukebox. The attached screen provides an associated film clip for the selected song. When Rick returns, I suggest to him that I will try it. Music by The Grateful Dead comes on, as does a video of their 'trucking' psychedelia. They combine in a way that feels packaged to comply with the machine. I wonder if 1992's fusion of sound and vision may be a limited gimmick that ends up relegated to a storeroom. Or, maybe my choice of track explains the void the video jukebox creates?

Finishing our beers, we exit the vacant mood in the back bar to embark on the short walk to Rick's house on Everton Street, only a few blocks away.

After making my departure, I experience a return to the sense of male destiny evoked by seeing *The Voyager*. Somewhere within the folds of intelligence and cosmic adversity, there must be a loitering female intent on soliciting romance, who stands up my alley, and has me in her vision. If this is a failed dream, then I can sustain the flailing gait of an alert *Talking Head,* spread-eagled exposure of a fallen *Lodger,* or the resolved outlook of an abandoned *Outsider.*

I've lived all over this town... I'm only thirty-five.

My workmates from the Wetlands Centre have signed a card during my days off. It is the density of the pleasant comments written like a floral arrangement across the inside that dearly captures me.

Happy Happy Birthday! Have a great day. Best Wishes Lou.

Geoff, another year has passed & you are now another year older!! Happy birthday!! Make the most of it before next year!! Have fun! Norma.

Another year! It's all right mate, I'm going grey too! Have a great day. Adam.

Well happy birthday a few days late! All the best for the year to come. Janine.

Dear Geoff. A special birthday wish for a special person. Thanks for all the special things you do. Anne.

All the special things I do. A secret acknowledgement of the errands that I have run enters my thoughts and is carried through the day. When it is time to leave work, their card, with its bright green aboriginal sea turtle motif, is carefully folded into an envelope for safe-keeping.

36   Thank You (Falettinme Be Mice Elf Agin)

The thick scab on the bridge of my nose is an extension of myself. My injury occupies only a small surface within the wider condition of the Northern Star's backroom, yet with each episode of stinging healing, every suspended moment in the bar seems to attach itself, and follow the course of my nose through space.

A few days earlier, I had evoked the promise of a walk to Pumpkin, our vigorous Blue Heeler. With the early spring daylight breathing apart curtains hung in the bedroom facing Oliver Street, her wriggling body could no longer contain its excitement and she leapt towards my tardy face. It may have been a jump intended to persuade with a lick, or to instigate by giving a sporting nip. For me, there was a question about whether I averted my head to tease or tether her. Canine incisors impacted and it still hurts as I enter the pub to see The Human Beings play their Thursday residency.

My explanation becomes honed in preparation to answer truthfully any enquiry about the appearance of my nose, but I must contend with a false account more likely taking precedence, such as that guy over there, who I sort of know, looks like he has been in a fight.

It is a testament to my social life that on this well-attended music night nobody approaches to share my birthday. This vague association with others lets the facts of my life become open to speculation. Because I've grown used to the dichotomy between what I know and what they believe, misinformation has become an accepted reality. As an extended flute solo lifts over-sophisticated jazz rhythms, I let myself surrender, resigned to looks askance and partial anonymity.

Joe Darling notices me as Rick's brother. Seen from across Rick's back fence or playing cricket with him on a City and Suburban field, Joe recognises me as an associate and acknowledges this with a nod. That is good enough for me!

37   The Real Old Mountain Dew

The makeshift residence lies ahead of us along an access road between fissured eucalypts on one side and, beyond a wire fence, the upper paddocks of the old farm. We unfasten the gate to enter the corner block that Mum and Dad retain as their stake on the land.

"Carnoustie" sits in the rolling hills of Quorrobolong. A cleared summit, crowned by a re-located railway carriage, is to the west. Tree-lined Sandy Creek along with the bluish heights of the Watagan Mountains are to the south. And the mahogany, spotted gum, and ironbark forests grow outward through "Al Halter's", and Dad's "The Links", to the north. They form an embrace around the large tin shed that stands open next to my parent's parked blue Mitsubishi Ute. And they create the scene that Gerard and I are slowly driving downhill into.

My parents have located their Millard caravan inside Dad's shed to connect to the power. A folding picnic table is erected in front of the open van. Mum is preparing chicken and salads for us. We gather at the table for a lunch which also consists of "the cake that men like" and soft drinks. Gerard is included in the tradition of dishing out the thickly caramel-iced fruitcake to males on the family's birthdays.

Because my friend and I are continuing on to the folk festival at Wollombi this afternoon, we politely refer to our pleasant meeting here as only a whistle-stop.

"Enjoy yourselves!" My parents say, in unison.

Gerard and I drive into the single-lane access road, and then turn on to Quorrobolong Road to the junction of Sandy Creek Road, and then through Ellalong, Paxton and Millfield, on to the historical village of Wollombi.

Toohey's Blue is a mid-strength beer, while Doctor Jurd's Jungle Juice is a mixture of strong wines and spirits produced locally. The Wollombi Tavern serves as its shopfront. Gerard remarks that the brew's eponym, a hairy face framed by grapes, bears a strong resemblance to my father. We have this discussion as we orientate on the tavern's timber verandah overlooking cattle-grazing grounds. We are drinking "Wombats", schooner glasses half-filled with beer and Jungle Juice. They are intoxicating, but the Tooheys Blue in mine does not mix, and the beverage tastes like *shit*. The image of a mound of fur stiffened beside a country road occurs to me. Lumbering wombats often suffer that fate around here.

When the sun sets on an Anglican church and a Catholic church, on a worn-down blacksmith's shed, on a hulking village barn, bannered streets, and tented venues, the following darkness brings with it a cold companion. This mountain chill is a resident who rudely reminds visitors to make necessary adjustments for a long night outside. The afternoon's sunny and sheltering warmth was a welcome respite from the symptoms of a flu, but the evening's plunge in temperature has unleashed a return of the barking cough.

Gerard and I share a table in the tavern's small restaurant.

An unused-to intensity in the kitchen may explain the flustered expression of our waitress? Or perhaps the crowded room of folkies, huddled in Friday night conversations, is the reason for her abruptness of movement? Mindfully, I blast another bout of downward coughs, feigning naivety that this could be the cause of her anxiety.

Gerard and I are each enjoying a fish meal.

I remark to my friend, seated across from me, "It's funny eating fish in a place that is so far from fishing."

While clearing phlegm from my throat, I entertain the thought of a refrigeration vehicle arriving at the pub with frozen supplies.

As you succumb to the demands of a flu, your conversation invariably becomes self-addressing. This is a natural consolation that usually expires with the onset of fever. Gerard's civil constitution is not disposed toward entertaining the likelihood of a friend's collapse during dinner. Instead, he engineers an incredulous support that goes so far as to suggest we order some dessert.

Practical thoughts on the freezing of ice cream are lost, interrupted by more coughs. My lips wipe across a folded serviette. Two bills settle separately in the drawer of a frowning cash register. And our patronage exits, to mutually sighed sounds of relief.

Passing festival-goers have, over time, shown me increasing concern. I have stood with them in short lines for shows. I have shared a 44-gallon fire-drum, drinking beer and making jovial remarks. But their closeness to my dogged cough has indubitably earned me, among them, a low regard. Gerard, too, appears more undecided about the value of my proximity. His availability seems to have withdrawn into the palls of smoke and incidents of sparks rising from the fire-drum between us. He has also involved himself in discussion with both the Clancy sisters. Their three-way conversation blends with the growing haze until I find myself alone.

The timber barn located at the back of the shop is open along one side. The stage therein hosts a band with a humorous name. Reels on Wheels play Irish music, specialising in that uplifting repertoire known to inspire leg movements that keep in time. The band members lean into their work. Dufty, pony-tailed and fair-haired, aligns himself over a fiddle.

The guitarist leads the band. On one side of his rhythmic strumming, a bodhrán player traps their beat and, on the other, a seated uilleann piper squeezes his instrument and pulls ridiculous expressions on his keen face. I throw caution aside and, regardless of reputation, leave my post at the drum, enter the dancing crowd, and join them perspiring wilfully!

38 Paperback Writer

I have been writing a diary since travelling to Far North
Queensland in August to visit Gemma, Arlo, and the kids.
The first *Largely* Literary Journal, with its caricature of Jack
Kerouac framed on the black and white cover, has almost
filled. And with the resolution made to continue writing
these accounts of daily life, I have added more copies,
reduced down from $12.95 to $4.95, then to $2.95, in a stock
clearance at Angus and Robertson's Hunter Street bookshop,
to the shelf. Stacked with the Kerouac diary are similar small
editions featuring Henry Lawson, Wolfgang Amadeus Mozart,
and J.R.R. Tolkien on their covers. Larger versions depict
Albert Einstein and Ned Kelly. The exaggerated portraits of
this worthy group provide sure invitation for further self-
expression. But home late after the theatre, I am reminded,
as my hands sleepily, soapily, clean dishes, that today's entry
for yesterday will have to wait until tomorrow night. Then
all of today's birthday can also be recorded. Instead, I venture further into the wet and cold realm of a stone cottage
in Ireland with Tim Winton's *The Riders*, held, wrapped in
green, beside my pillow in bed.

"Would you like to see a play called *The Human Behan* this
Saturday night on my birthday?" I ask Gerard who is sitting
opposite me at a very low table. With his interest in the
stuffy warmth of the Turkish restaurant registering as open
eyes, I continue before he replies. "It's about the Irish writer
Brendan Behan. The actor playing him is Bob Ellis. It's on at
the Mission Theatre in King Street."

The invitation works. Gerard agrees to go. "Sounds good Geoff," he says, in a voice lulled by Guinness and the discomfort of his long legs seated cross-legged.

On Gerard's 34th birthday his meal is a lamb pizza and mine is vegetarian. We divide the bill where we pay, at the rear of the cooking-servery area. Our waitress has a mass of curly hair, an Arabic nose, and exotic eyes. Her vest is embroidered with a Middle-Eastern design.

"She belly dances here," my friend shares as we exit onto Beaumont Street.

"She works in Nina's supermarket too," I offer in agreement.

The two of us walk in the same direction. Toward our homes located mere streets apart from each other in Hamilton.

9th September 1995

Waking to the sounds of morning bird songs outside my window. Vote in the local council election, The Greens, Margaret Goumas, and Greg Heys. What a way to spend my birthday I think as I don a raincoat at Sandgate Station. Plentiful worms to feed the display tanks, the short-necked turtle grabs a few. Surprised to recognise the groom at today's Wetlands Centre wedding from earlier this morning en route to the bread shop. Serenaded by a bagpiper. Making your private love a public vow. 'The Teddy Bears' Picnic' as a finale on the pipes. Doing barrow-loads of sand. Paddy gives me a casuarina to plant on the avenue. A young hippy-type assures me I'll make it as I run for the homeward train. Walking into the big yellow sun down Donald Street. Phoned by Gemma (her friend Kay's a fan of mine), Mum and Dad, Kerry Rose sings "Happy Birthday" while Rick follows to say they're thinking of me. Watch the shining white full moon rising through clouds... (I close on Kerouac's bulbous forehead, choose Henry Lawson's upturned moustache, and continue writing)... before departing to Gerard's. He gives me a *Fuse Box* CD, gift-wrapped, with its receipt thankfully. At the theatre, Bob Ellis's total effort in portraying Brendan Behan, truly a soak. Tim Richards performs boldly in a blue singlet as Bob's younger half. The lead's costume is a baggy tan suit, yellow shirt, and emerald green tie. The good woman Beatrice has thick red hair. Irish accents in the foyer, from County Kerry to this listener's ear. Under a wave of tiredness, I lose the plot in the second act. Afterwards, a peek into the Town Hall where today's voting is being counted after having visited the toilet where Prince Charles would have pissed. Telling Gerard my new joke. "If brains were glue – you wouldn't have enough to stick your finger up your arse!" Taking *Fuse Box* home to exchange. Dishwashing duty, then reading in bed.

39   Lifeboat Party

Hubert's green Renault, parked outside his Hamilton home, encourages me to pay him a visit. My Oliver Street neighbour has his birthday the day before mine, on the eighth of September.

I am greeted at the Raymonds' alcove doorway with their usual hospitality. Hubert and Bianca spread out along their plush leather-upholstered lounge. It is a school night, so the girls have already retreated to their bedrooms while Luther sleeps in his junior room out the back. We keep our voices subdued as we enjoy cold Resch's beers taken from the fridge. My married friends have nothing to prove and are relaxed at this hour when the family is in dock. I occupy a large cushioned comfortable chair under the window as we sit passively in the glow and murmur of the television.

The ABC is screening Dennis Potter's last scripted show, *Cold Lazarus*. He died in May from a cancer that he candidly named 'Rupert' after Mr Murdoch's cultural invasion of the British media. It is the end of the series. The Raymonds share a trained involvement with the story, quietly taking it in. I am aware of a heightened consciousness invested in the programme and its stimulation when meanings overlap. Rather stunned by the show and the others' silence, I make a sleepy and gentle farewell met by Hubert and Bianca's contented acknowledgement.

My birthday evening is a party at home with myself. I indulge in stubbies of Rainier beer, an American lager brewed near Seattle that features Washington's highest mount, Rainier, on its label.

A CD recording of Van Morrison's *A Night in San Francisco* holds court at an elevated volume. I am aware of my identifying world becoming enacted on the stage between the windowed kitchen and the musty-carpeted dining room. Van's energy is unrelenting. The songs segue. Guests come and go in mantras of acclamation.

"Candy Dulfer! Candy Dulfer!"

"Teena Lyle! Teena Lyle!"

"Jimmy Witherspoon! Jimmy Witherspoon!"

"The king of the blues! John Lee Hooker! John Lee Hooker!!"

Was there any doubt? Is there any doubt? Van is the man! Van is the man!

My feelings are captured by solos from brass, percussion, keyboard, mouth harp and electric guitar. They are rendered tender by soulful vocals. I have become the music I am hearing. Yet, without an audience for this celebration of personal being, my vow to receive only incoming calls lies defeated.

Tonight's drunken injection surely dies unless I share the glory!

Thus, the merry propulsion stalls as Van's sounds are made mute *en route* to the seated phone.

"Hello, Aunty Ruth? It's Geoffrey. I just thought I would phone you to let you wish me a happy birthday."

"Well of course, Geoffrey, happy birthday. This is unexpected! It usually goes the other way around, I am supposed to ring you. I thought you might be out celebrating tonight with your friends."

"No, I am just alone at home."

I am conscious of the slurred words and automatically experience shame, for Aunty Ruth would be unused to drunkenness. I tactfully reach for a topic framed in ordinariness.

"Have you heard from Mum and Dad and Aunty Ray, I mean Aunty Mary, and Uncle Ray?"

"Well, not yet."

"Yes, I suppose it's too early to get a postcard. They're making their way north from California up to Canada."

I think about the deal we made at the airport, to collect a souvenir from Mount Rainier!

What happens now, in not mentioning that I've been drinking, in the emptiness surrounding my end of the conversation, is an affliction of self-wonder.

I find consolation in Aunty Ruth's dignified speech patterns.

"... We went to Berrima on a bus trip... a pleasant little town... I've never seen so many antique shops... Have you been there?"

"Yes, I hitch-hiked through there on my way to visit Gemma and Arlo. I can remember those antique shops, they had verandahs, but I was just passing through at the time. I might have stopped to buy a cold drink from one. Did you go to the gaol, Aunty Ruth?"

"No, they don't take visitors. They still have prisoners in there, you know?"

"Oh, yeah, right. I guess you'd only visit them if you were related. Well, Aunty Ruth, I'd better get back to... um, I'm feeling pretty tired now, I might call it a day soon. Do you think you will make it up to Nelson Bay for Christmas?"

"It is a bit early to tell yet, Geoffrey."

"Of course. Well, I hope you can. But we'll probably see each other when Mum and Dad and Aunty Mary and Uncle Ray come back from America."

"When is that, do you know?"

"Oh, I think it is in mid to late October. It was good seeing you and Aunty Lola at the airport."

I think about how my visit to Sydney turned out, that notorious dirty weekend. Is there no train of thought I can complete?

"You sound tired, Geoffrey. Have you been working today?"

"Yes, I am still at the Wetlands Centre. Anyway, I'd better get to bed... I'm starting to lose concentration."

I am starting to lose concentration.

"Good night, dear. Thank you for calling me, even if it is the wrong way around."

When I stand, my head spins a little from lack of circulation. My night has not ended, but the party's over and the guests have left. I am conflicted about this undermining action. Aunty Ruth is dear to me, however, her invitation to the celebration was not necessarily warranted.

A *Night in San Francisco* stays inserted on the carousel of my Philips midi-system, having been turned off with an emphatically depressed button. The three empties collide with each other in the recycle bin. An unattended auditorium looks blankly through my kitchen window from under subdued street lighting. A stream of urine, speaking to housed water, echoes inside the slightly grotty toilet bowl. With a flush. That's how the world ends!

The phone rings, an incoming call, before work. I grapple with its antiquated handset, the earpiece and mouthpiece jut roundly into their respective positions. I am surprised to hear Mum's voice.

"Geoffrey, it's your Mum. We are in San Francisco."

Her voice infiltrates the residual determination of a disappointed morning, and diffuses it. I inform her about coincidentally playing Van Morrison's concert from the same city. She accounts that it is the most-like-an-Australian-city she's been in, and that it instils her with a sense of ease. I am buoyed by her connection. Rick is mentioned. "He is giving me a lift out to Wollombi for the folk festival this Friday afternoon." And I close with, "I will... and my love to all of you, too."

40 I Put a Spell on You

Steve has volunteered at the Wetlands Centre with skilful energy. His tanned, lanky body and practical ability have combined in an effort that stands apart. Not only does Steve set an example, this owner-builder from Tuggerah has a way of delivering disarming insights.

"Are you pissed?"

I keep up my pace, while wondering whether Steve means the three Rainier beers I drank last night? Or does he think I am disgruntled because we are working together?

He has brought along his duck-feeder and rat-catching shelter. There's no doubt that Steve's construction methods are sound. And the useful invention sets the standard for how the ducks are to be fed and the rats are to get caught. He is entitled to feel proud about the structure he has made, a *very* useful duck-feeder and rat-catching shelter transported from his renovated home on Tuggerah Lake.

It is a sunny spring day, the kind of day when work gets done well, although, being my fortieth birthday, makes it special too, and it is understood we will all take a break from work for morning tea with me in mind.

We take our seats around a table in the Visitors Centre café overlooking BHP Pond, soaking up the sunlight just as I am soaking up the attention given by the thoughtful staff sharing tea and coffee and the sweet slices purchased on the way to work by someone kind-hearted.

I explain that I am going to see Donovan at the Basement in Sydney tonight, and this requires having a half-day off. The travel time home to shower and dress, then catch an afternoon train to Sydney, will take the rest of the day.

That Donovan sang 'Mellow Yellow' is not known to my workmates, so I try singing the opening lines of 'Catch the Wind'. "In the chilly hours and minutes of uncertainty, I long to be, in the warm arms of your love and mine... aah but I might as well try and catch the wind."

Cheree sitting at the table, listens, as do the others, with generosity. I know it is a good song that they should like, but I am not sure my rendition does it justice.

As my heart yearns for the stuff of love in Donovan's song, there is romance in the air.

Cheree's voice speaks a single word, the word is *friendship*.

I hear her say this, only in my head from her head, but I am not sure Cheree has said anything telepathically.

Later at lunch, Andrew approaches me with a heartfelt apology. He did not know that it was my birthday when he missed the morning tea. Andrew's acknowledgment is unconditional and not defined by his position as CEO. Soon after, the afternoon opens a wide door, away from the duties of employment towards adventure.

I arrive at Circular Quay and breathe in the welcoming air.

I decide to eat a congratulatory meal in a restaurant addressing the ferry wharves. My waitress here exudes confidence from her breasts, eyes, crutch, and curvy behind. I satisfy myself with a tangy, fleshy baked fish dish and fantasise about the menu the comely waitress withholds. Welcome to the year of the bare midriff.

The Basement is reached via a laneway entrance and then down a flight of stairs to a subterranean foyer.

My first beer is beside an angular, bearded man who is slightly younger than me. He is sunk into an outlook that, while being aware of the scene around him, seems to draw its bearings from an environment located somewhere else. The orientation of the lone drinker evokes a familiar allure, he reminds me of Richard Burton. I sense that he might offer a safe haven from the mid-week punters, however, I cannot make conversation here, so I opt, instead, to explore outside his watchful harbour.

I encounter a row of ticket-holders gathering, with their drinks, along a terrace that overlooks the booked-seat diners at tables that front the stage. All are in a hub of servicing and socialising. A landing between the upper viewers and lower viewers acts as floor space for those who may later decide to lean themselves into the performance.

A young man stands out. He has taken the trouble to dress in imitation of Donovan on the cover of A *Gift from a Flower to a Garden*. With a long floral jacket and a single stemmed flower, and his hair cut like Donovan, he passes me as part of a time-warped parade. He looks too young to have experienced the eleven albums I collected as a teen.

Catch the Wind... Universal Soldier... Sunshine Superman... Mellow Yellow... A Gift from a Flower to a Garden... Hurdy Gurdy Man... Barabajagal... Open Road... Cosmic Wheels... Essence to Essence... 7-Tease.

Or to have a memory of an evening when a thunderstorm broke across the lake at Eleebana and I fed my youthful thrill by turning the sitar and quivering baritone of 'Hurdy Gurdy Man' up loud to match the sound of the tempest outside. Or for remembering when I gave a fond hand to Deidre in shared reverence for the cross-legged troubadour sitting before us in spiritual white at the Civic Theatre in 1975. Or for our surprise at his bad-mouthing technical faults, "fucking mechanical monsters," in an angry Scottish brogue.

Next to the Donovan mythology I am honouring, the young man's show of fandom poses awkwardly.

A middle-aged male voice-over introduces the supporting act as a singer standing on the ladder to success, though her name is lost in the garbled hype. She has a voice that is nuanced and potent, and her effort-driven showcase is stirring. She strums her guitar with vigour and talent, and she is attractive. In a music scene I know little of, I wonder where this trajectory will land her?

There is though, a rising sense that the young singer's solid set has spanned into the special time reserved for Donovan. Descending on me is an uneasy awareness of Donovan's late arrival, of hours already used and the night going over schedule, and the venue becoming too crowded.

"The gift from a flower to a garden" is obscured in a veil of cigarette smoke and the shadows of silhouetted punters. A woman nearby faints to the floor, her prone figure is attended to within the chattering crowd. Even time herself folds on stiff knees and falls to a slow tolling of stale air.

Not until the eleventh hour does Donovan reach the microphone and chair. His somewhat bedraggled, much-older, countenance bears an expression of pleasure to be here. His long, grey, wavy hair frames a morose, yet grateful, face. His eyes seem to see for miles. He greets us as he hunches over an emerald-green acoustic guitar.

When Donovan sings, a shudder on a sublime frequency passes through the crowd. I feel my mythology nurtured, and time deconstruct, familiar moments from treasured recordings are reborn in the voice and tripping fingers of the troubadour incarnate.

Donovan gives us a way to roll away the claustrophobic stone of mass capacity and exhaled nicotine. Another woman falls to the floor. As if an epidemic has fallen upon us, the set list become a valiant recourse against coma.

"You can have too much nostalgia."

I agree with the fellow listener. Too much nostalgia can make you nauseous. Like a patchwork poncho woven to suit a beaten generation, Donovan's magic carpet is losing us. We are unable to escape the too-close basement on the rungs he bestows, even though we dearly try.

A fire door at the other side of the venue has been set ajar. An intelligent crowd stands apart from the strange brew of stretched necks in the room. I am behind two dark-skinned ladies whose bodies are based in better times. I imbibe their feminine poise, and I receive their combined closeness with more meaning than a view of Donovan, although I ache for the troubadour in his time now out of reach. We are near the end of the show.

The houselights come on.

Exit Door.

I am with a group of people who have found grace in breathing normally. I follow them onto Pitt Street and into sanity.

I lie awake in the CB Hotel in empty turmoil, my ceremonial admission to middle age dying in solitary confinement. There's something missing, about true love not idol worship, about a body without another in an uneven bed. The window beside me is partly open to the well between the lives of others and mine, and I'm thinking, should I've stayed home instead, received, for certain, a visit from Rick? It is enough, isn't it? The city hushes me towards oblivion.

I am taking a morning walk past the Chinese Gardens when I notice the frame and intent of Tony Brown, also walking.

I haven't seen him since we were in the surf together off Dixon Park on Australia Day in 1988. Since the Coles off Hunter Street when he introduced me to his new wife. We once exchanged records, my Suzi Quatro for his Daddy Cool, back at his home in Eleebana after school. He once shot me in the hand with a split-pea, leaving a permanent imprint.

We come together in a handshake, and in recognition of our near 40th birthdays.

"Yours and mine are only four days apart."

In a bigger mode of meeting, where selves keep a pact to reconcile the genius of values with the lives we lead, our conversation agrees to continue later, outside Tony's workplace on Sussex Street.

"At around two-thirty."

"I'm driving back to Newcastle this arvo Nick-o, I can give you a lift home."

41   Cross-Eyed and Painless

The fact that a bare number of my fellow employees have attended the birthday afternoon tea makes me awkwardly aware that I may be a peripheral entity. One of them, seated at the table with unoccupied chairs, explains.

"We couldn't all make it because they've found something interesting on the computer."

I recognise this is meant to validate their collective absence, but to find purpose in a random distraction, and one that substitutes the importance of my birthday, shows a communal lack of caring.

I am bothered that I had not asked the consultancy team to join me. Had I, perhaps I would not be feeling so overlooked at my celebration? Their office can be seen opposite.

Beyond the Visitors Centre, the BHP Pond summons a sense of workplace. I am best served by re-entering that world.

Formed in a crude circle, the energy of learning songs passes through our congregation. In an upstairs room with ample windows, a high ceiling, and a single cross on the wall, we are aspiring to channel African American gospel.

After singing, it is our habit to meet at Giannotti's café, located in the last busy block of Beaumont Street. Jacki, who leads us in song, uses this rendezvous to visit her sister who waitresses here. I have since discovered a taste for bruschetta.

There's a bond of togetherness at our chosen tables, and a tolerance towards those who arrive late, "looking for a park", or who must leave early to drive home. In this conference of hearts and minds, there are moments that invite individual attention. Jacki's leading mouth opens sufficiently to invite me, yet I do not take the opportunity to announce that it is my birthday.

Betsy announces she has plans to soldier on to the Northern Star, which would suit my aim to celebrate my birthday indeed, only I have vowed to meet Gerard at home for a beer.

He informs me he had gone to the café, but was unable to see me there. I try to quell my sense of defeat in his quiet, smallish, lounge-room, on an uncomfortable armchair, in the umbrella glow of the lamp stand. We toast my birthday with a strong beer that doesn't suit my taste. There's an uncountable conclusion of occupying the wrong space. As if this is an act of duty that has no meaning.

The vacuum persists as I stand, conscious of indifference and Betsy's absence, among the night crowd in the back room of the Northern Star.

With my heart breaking in wanting to share the day, I return to the emptiness of my own house.

Across the street, Hubert's Renault pulls in gently outside the sanctuary of his home, the soft heartbeat of family life emanates from the lounge-room light. It is after 11pm and Hubert's afternoon shift at James Fletcher Hospital has ended. The hospitality of the Raymonds is peerless and I have knocked on their door at this time before and received a cordial, albeit slightly bemused, reception. However, on this night, when it matters more than most to feel relevant, I cannot perform such an intrusion into their lives.

A solitary walk takes me to Gregson Park, to sit alone in the silent address of an empty view. It is midnight, and I feel terrible. I make an inner resolve to seek the assistance of a psychiatrist.

42   Our House

The house where I live in Oliver Street is quite ordinary on the outside. The walls are composed of a non-descript weathered white cladding material. When you push on its surface, the compression indicates an air pocket between the weatherboards underneath and a bland makeover. An aluminium awning above the bedroom windows is curved, half-blind to the street facing it. The two front steps are inside an alcove part-way down the side of the house.

I bring my bike in through the opened door. Arlo and Dad are sitting expectantly in the down-market lounge-room. Arlo occupies the second-hand lounge with unforgiving angular armrests while Dad is propped up in the recliner I secured from Gerard's parents when they were up-sizing. The way he holds his arms outstretched along the rests suggests he is on the verge of leaving. Arlo appears tense from sharing this time and space with his father-in-law. Both make the same announcement when I enter. They are here to join me for dinner at Pasta at the Pub in celebration of my birthday.

Arlo adds, "Peg will be joining us there. She just lives around the corner."

Gerard, and our friend Melissa, are also to be included.

My bedroom is at the front of the house. By the time I have showered, dressed again, and re-entered the lounge-room, today's news is screening.

The small 18-inch NEC portable occupies a central location along the wall. Not long after I settle, the broadcast gives an update on the atrocities unfolding in East Timor. More footage of innocent citizens seeking independence from Indonesia's tyrannical military regime under attack from maniacal armed vigilantes turns to a slanted report against the island's Catholic Archbishop. Dad reacts to the church leader's apparent hypocrisy with an outburst that his support for the popular movement is deluded, and, by association, their claims for justice are a mockery. I am aggrieved by Dad's criticism which goes to the heart of their cause. I see red.

"You can't say that. There are people being murdered by the Indonesians. How can you say that and support the Indonesians?"

Dad takes offense and glowers. Arlo does not comment because he does not want to get involved in our conflict.

"I can't go out to dinner with you," I add.

The phone is in the entrance hallway inside the front door. It sits on a table with a shelf for the phonebook and a small cupboard underneath. Arlo has left to stay the night at Peg's and Dad has driven off in his car. I call Gerard to explain that I have called the dinner off.

"I've had an argument with Dad about East Timor."

Gerard accepts the decision with disappointment. And offers to notify Melissa.

Melissa calls. She urges that just the three of us, "the Virgos", could still make it an outing, as we have done in recent years. She pledges heartfelt help in any way but I decline her offer of assistance.

The kitchen looks out onto the street and the vacant parking space. Through the open window the world can see a single man preparing another dinner on his own. But the world no longer has any interest in me tonight.

The food is forced down against churning emotion.

I am acutely aware of alienating my friends.

Well into the night, Dad does not return to the spare bedroom.

Once awake, I am unsettled by the stillness in the room left empty by Dad. There is no sign of his bag on the floor and no sign of his car parked outside.

When I call Mum with a personal need to explain my battle with Dad, whatever knowledge we hold of today being a birthday, is overlooked. Mum's tone is matter-of-fact.

"He slept over at the other house and came home this morning... Are you off to work today?"

And, although she wishes me a happy birthday, the pity of what is not said, and cannot be said, outweighs any special identification of the day.

My job at the Wetlands is called General Assistant. Most of my work is out in the grounds, mowing the walking trails, picnic and entrance areas and slashing the fire trail. Trudi is the Visitors Centre manager. She observes a record of all the staff's birthdates, and volunteers for the duty of organising a cake. But her gesture today goes refused in a quandary over self-worth.

"Thanks. But I'd rather that you didn't recognise my birthday today... I'll just work through."

When Gerard first became my friend, I thought our companionship ill-suited and bound to diverge, however his persistence, and my acceptance, have, over time, forged a bond we both endeavour to sustain. Gerard's visit after work today typifies this conscientious effort. His welcome entrance celebrates my birthday. He is carrying two cans of imported beer.

"I was surprised to see these in the bottle shop. Boddington's was one of my favourites in Bristol."

I say I like their images of bees, and ask if they are honey-flavoured.

"They're not as bitter as a lot of lagers. But let's try them and see. Cheers, Geoff!"

43   One is the Loneliest Number

Loneliness is a strange thing...
It creeps up behind you like an ominous shadow,
engulfs, and captures, never letting go...
it's walking through a void,
hearing your own footsteps,
making sense of your troubled thoughts...
I am lonely.
And alone I walk.

Lines from this poem, 'Loneliness', loiter on a Saturday morning, giving it an edge, even though they have come to empty moods since we lived in Canada. As a teenager, robed in wide flares and a loose nylon spray jacket, I used to traverse the halls of Avalon Junior High with much the same confidence as any 14-year-old. I had friends and good looks, yet something set me apart, a disposition I thought recognised by some of my teachers, especially Mrs Scheelar, whose eyes looked deeply into mine.

I have lived alone for a number of years. A lady once asked me whether I ever got lonely, and I replied not really, thinking that you can become used to separateness.

Back in the earlier days of my parents' time at Quorrobolong, it became obvious to me that I needed to relate to a person other than Mum or Dad. Most of my friends had supernaturally disappeared in the mist of a departing flying saucer, or onboard the refrain of a slowly dis-berthing ship in a dream. Only Keith had made a return.

His occupancy in a suburb near where I lived in town led to a renewal of our ties. Sharing a queue into the Palais night-club, even a dance floor at Tubemakers, but more so regular visits from me, consolidated our reunion. I sat and chatted confidently while he repaired a motorcycle, for example. Perhaps we had a dogged nostalgia for our first shared house in Shortland? Or a common respect for a friendship discovered outside the rules of society? As I bothered on Mum and Dad's verandah about having a friend to whom I could confirm I was real, a pressing urge to invite Keith dawned on me, and rose paramount.

A precedent for making timely contact with Keith was present in the struggle I once had with a public phone in Parnell Place. I was a resident of Newcastle East at the time. The recollection of desperation mixed with shame inhabiting the booth as I dialled his number has stayed with me over the years. One time, in a house I was visiting, a musician who was living alone put down his saxophone and stood vulnerable before us in order to let us know he was lonely. I remember his public admission making me more uncomfortable than sympathetic. I battled this discomfort when I spoke over my hypocrisy and let Keith hear what I meant to say.

These complicated feelings for making contact experienced in the mid 1980s re-emerged with the decision to reach out from the farm. However, their demands had increased over the years since and overwhelmed my bid to approach the phone in the farmhouse hall. I answered the challenge to myself to invite Keith with the dissuasion that we were too far out of the city at Quorrobolong for him to visit. I rode my pushbike to Neath instead and explored backroads from the station on my own, albeit accompanied by Keith's apparition, which I believed would have appreciated the local bushland.

Keith had become symbolic of declaring allegiance, and I had struggled with being consistent in this area.

Another time, on a balmy evening, I'd ridden past his front door without knocking, only to come across a badly bashed bloke near Waratah Station. His story was he had been mugged, kicked in the back, and left lying on the roadside. An ambulance had been called. I stayed with him and talked until it arrived then left him to their care. Although there was much to discuss with Keith about this episode so close to his doorstep, I persuaded myself to pedal past again.

Because escaping loneliness is optimal, I dial 49671977 from my hall phone and listen to the ring tone until Keith answers.

"It's my birthday today... would you mind if I came over for a visit... it would be better than spending it on my own."

"Sure, mate. Come on over."

Climbing into Keith's passenger side is like getting into the cockpit of a stock car. The seat is bracketed onto the chassis and fixed well back from the dashboard. Buckling into this modified bucket readies me for road travel tailored to the impulses of a self-confessed rev-head. As I take in the view from the carport across the vast lawn to the renovations at the back of his house, Keith operates the sliding bolt which releases his corrugated tin gate from the fence, and allows him to swing it inwards along the arced concrete path on its fitted dolly wheel. It makes a comforting cranking sound as it turns on its hinges. We reverse into the lane, where I sit again in solitude as Keith shuts the gate. Once he re-occupies the driver's seat, the car's engine rumbles and we commence along the route under overhanging branches and between back fences to the turn onto Hanbury Street.

Keith has offered to drive me over to Hamilton for my folk club committee meeting this afternoon.

My attendance at the meeting is due to a sense of duty. I am an office bearer. I have completed the design for the posters using cartoonish bush dancers and posted them on windows and noticeboards at select locations. But in the company of the people around me my loyalty is not truly felt. I long for the ease of the time I spent with Keith this afternoon, our casual conversation versus my current alienation. His reaction to my decision to attend a formal meeting rather than celebrate my birthday was one of bemusement.

Now I must comply with protocols and procedures.

"The minutes of the last meeting... "

"Business arising from the minutes of the last meeting... "

"Agenda items for this meeting... "

This language lacks humour, and I wonder where the comradery and musicality are, the folksiness?

The committee members have returned to the Wesley Hall after a break for dinner. Some have set the supper tables in the kitchen, while others have arranged chairs around the perimeter of the dance floor. Those who believe their roles are to stand at the door have taken their place and another two are helping the bush band set up.

A man, whose name I can't remember, occupies the hall with a command for attention. I resist this with an ironic gait, but once I am within striking range he stakes his claim.

"Hi Geoff."

His puzzling, overly-familiar, keen and countrified expression looms above my head.

"It's Lester. You mean to tell me you really don't know?"

As if to compensate for my lack of memory, I make a concerted effort to familiarise myself with aspects of his identity.

"I do small building jobs for people in my area."

"The long drive into town…"

"I don't eat very much."

"I'm thinking of selling the place."

The sound of a fiddle soars briefly through the speakers, then initiates a tune, bringing true movement to legs that have hovered too long in disingenuousness.

Lester embarks in pursuit of a partner for the first dance.

My partner for the next dance is willing, she and I can hold hands and I can encircle her waist. We can raise our arms in promenade or navigate our feet to the caller's routeing, dutiful toward our sets, cheerfully obedient about handing on to a new partner when the dancing is progressive, meeting and greeting, coming together again before running the merry gauntlet.

My legs are liberated, and even though my desires may be compromised, I cannot complain about what the polished wooden floor has supported tonight.

44   The Irish Rover

Sunday mornings on Beaumont Street allow more space for the ways people mean to walk. It is not that there is less meaning in their direction, there's just a broader sense of purpose.

I remember Michael from those heady nights in the back room of the Northern Star. Plunking adamantly on his electric bass while Shaun thrashed the drums, and Peter's guitar strummed sympathetically with Steve's banjo and vocals with an Irish brogue. Three years later, that tuneful recollection of Tinker's Curse adds a dose of verve to this moment of mutual recognition.

"Hello Michael."

"Hello Geoff," he politely replies.

"Are you playing any music these days?" I ask him.

"I'm doing some solo work, guitar and vocals."

I think about how his appearance has changed, how the long hair of the reserved bassist has, along with those earlier and younger days, receded. He couldn't be quieter, but nowadays the more mature Michael wears, above a mildly rounder face, noticeably shorter hair. The times I have seen him slightly bent over the counter at Maclean's Bookshop have left an image of him at home in the realm of books.

Our local is the Kent Hotel. Gerard and I joke that we don't need to dress up to drink here because we're locals. We make our way through the swinging front door straight to the bar with its line of taps. I feel a mutual bond with him. His offer to shout the first round, on this day, the ninth of September

2001, is savoured, while the time it takes for our beer to swirl and fill two schooners stands religiously still.

As locals, and Virgos by nature, we have preferred locations when it comes to taking our seats. Lately this has been the singular table and two chairs mounted on the stage beside the pool table. From here, a view of the entire front bar is available. After the customary cheers, our attention turns to each other.

This afternoon, about 5pm, I latch onto Gerard's closeness and conversation with some determination. Apart from my friend, there is another man also looking to know me. Seated in the company of strangers, I recognise Darrel, yet elect to remain oblivious to his stare. There is too much discontent in Darrel's argument with the world, which isn't helped by his drunkenness. We have spoken walking up Sandgate Road, at the station and the one time he visited the Wetlands. I remember the quarrel in his manner. In my eyes, his status is Fulva's ex, and I believe she should be able to move on in her life.

Gerard and I make our way out, across the pedestrian crossing and beside the vast bare wall on the Cleary Street corner. In late afternoon light, and a bit drunk, we part shaking hands firmly in front of Gerard's. Across the road, in the Salvation Army building, a tuning of brass instruments can just be heard.

45   I'm a Boy

"Happy birthday to you... Happy birthday to you... Happy birthday dear Geoffrey," (in the background, "Uncle Geoffrey") "... Happy birthday to you," dragged out with a discordant howl.

Gemma is the mother hen. Her clutch of three clucky chickens, truly cute and a little crazy, gather under her umbrella wings to join her in this tuneless serenade on my answering machine. Probably performed before they took the hilly walk out to meet the school bus on the Promised Land Loop Road, their message is sufficient to bring a sense of belonging and purpose to my day.

Keith arrives around mid-day to take up my invitation for lunch. He parks his metallic blue Ford station-wagon out front and knock knocks on the door.

We decide on going up the street to grab a sandwich from the Subway outlet at the Oasis. It is nice weather for a walk, sharing the path, chatting while we stroll. At the junction with Beaumont Street, I keep to my correct cautious route of passing around the three crossings of the intersection in order to cross the road. The Oasis is open and airy, even if the cast metal table and bench seats are uncomfortable underneath. We eat and drink rather quickly.

The walk back to Oliver Street is at much the same pace as before, only in the opposite direction.

We climb into Keith's car for the drive out to the Hoyts Cinema at Charlestown. I am keeping with a little tradition of seeing a film on my birthday. The alignment of movies and times has resulted in the favourably reviewed *About a Boy*, starring Hugh Grant.

As Keith cannot abide Hugh Grant, he delivers me to the hill-top carpark and lets me exit the car and enter the cinema on my own.

Standing outside afterwards, I feel as though I am occupying a space informed by the film's emotional intelligence. Hugh Grant acted well, showing how much the character's relationship with a teenage boy mattered to him.

Homeward on a Charlestown bus, I carry the satisfaction of having fulfilled an identifying ritual on my birthday. I have empathised with Hugh Grant's surprise at finding out that his middle-aged bachelor could become a friend to a much younger boy, even though it was truly about getting a girl. It's a self-realisation I will likely keep to myself, too.

46   The Light Pours Out of Me

I cross the mown lawn toward Neil with a steady movement of arms and legs, a straight back, sure torso, and a handsome manner. Neil Longbottom has become a stalwart at The Wetlands Centre. His lanky, tanned limbs are ever active at maintenance tasks, like weeding the sensory trail path. Neil and I have not seen eye to eye at times, but for the sake of job satisfaction, we keep a mutual respect. He stands in a royal-blue issue polo shirt with a logo depicting an array of water-bird feet embroidered above his tanned left tit, and a floppy white hat. There are no guns drawn as we approach each other. There is a pact of inner confidence. And I will remember this as a day when I walked tall.

Lock up at the end of the day is a kind of ballet. Roller doors fall, shut and lock, gates swing together with chain and padlock, doors downstairs and upstairs close and lock, alarms are set. I take my time, the train leaves on the hour, usually six o'clock. I have the place to myself, just on dusk, I depart on foot. A ring-tailed possum suddenly moves along a trunk, stops and turns, facing me, its nocturnal eyes nakedly open.

Gerard and Tianshu arrive at my home in the evening. They ceremoniously present a framed photograph of Nobby's lighthouse and breakwater. A dark cardboard edge gives the lucid image a letter-box effect. This iconic Newcastle location is represented in a myriad of ways. I have an impressionist Paul Haggith painting, found face-down on a disused studio floor, on my lounge-room wall, for example. I notice that Tianshu and Gerard operate as one. Their birthday visit expresses a shared commitment, given as an unconditional gesture, it conveys a message of their newfound coupling.

The next day, I somehow manage to overlook my work keys. They are set down inside the building when the back door is pulled shut. Not only the keys, but also my wallet, railway ticket, and means of currency for the coming weekend are locked in. Fortunately I can call on Norma, who is housed on the hill behind the wetlands, to borrow an entry key. She is due in tomorrow to continue transferring information about the Freckled Ducks onto a computer with Allan's help, so I can return the keys to her then.

Norma interrupts a domestic scene in her Mort Street home to assist me. I make a grateful departure, through her native garden haven, carefully open and close the access gate and re-enter the neighbouring parkland.

A stand of *Melaleuca nodosa* makes an obscure web of shadows where I negotiate the downhill track. On the hillside below, an open view of a body of water, bordered by clumps of tree crowns, is irradiated by a gross full moon. I feel privileged to be on my own, walking into a world guided by a referencing, ethereal light.

I make the following day's journey to return the keys in a strong wind. As expected, Norma can be found at work in the centre's office, immersed in her responsibilities. I relate to her the magic of yesterday's moon, and she responds with a characteristic inward glow.

Visiting Keith on the way home another, internal, wind calls. With quickened language, I inform him, "I'd better get going. I've got a ticket to see Lou Reed at the Civic Theatre tonight." Sympathetic to the urgency, Keith offers to drive me home, making my panic more bearable.

Left alone in my kitchen, I face a conundrum over the amount of ingredients to cook and the time left to consume them.

The crowded foyer of the Civic Theatre is peopled with connectivity. Occupying the ornamental room, the punters are luxurious in their raised awareness. This is the threshold of a realm that's more than ordinary, it's rock and roll. I gather composure sufficiently to ask for a rum and coke.

Hubert Raymond is here, already tanked after drinking at the Clarendon with his mates. Bright-eyed and fraternal, they are ready to take their seats, middle row and near the stage.

My seat is one from the aisle. A fair way back, however, with an over-all view.

I see Yoga Julie's husband, Jenko, working through the crowd.

The fellow next to me interrupts my train of thought. He is a fan. He tells me facts about Lou Reed's life, his music, and his recordings. I find him rectifying.

An excitable couple sits in front of us, wriggling and speaking as if on the brink of sexual intercourse.

Soon the great band walks on stage. Each member noiselessly addresses their instruments and means of amplification.

Lou commences an iconic Velvet Underground riff, then pauses his guitar, "A lot of people say 'Sweet Jane' has just two chords. But if you listen closely..."

He plays the intro to 'Sweet Jane' again, "That's right! There's a little strum at the end. That's what makes it sound..."

He plays it again, "You see? Now, I'm not gonna play the song."

The audience emits a collective moan, before Lou and the band launch into a heartfelt version of 'Men of Good Fortune'.

Again he adopts a conversational manner, "Hey, Fernando, I didn't know you were playing the piano."

Fernando demonstrates a few notes on the bass, creating a keyboard effect enjoyed by his friendly questioner.

Lou's back is straight, with a strap across one shoulder, he wields the guitar in front of him as he turns to talk or to start up another song. The band is rhythmic and soaring.

Further in, Lou asks the audience if Newcastle is a small town. To those who reply in the affirmative, he barks good-naturedly, "Well then, why don't you fucking leave?"

I notice a dumpy, crew-cut, young man standing to the side of the stage. He moves in a sensitive, self-conscious way, at times contributing high harmonising vocals.

Lou gestures, "Now... I'd like to introduce my tai chi master..."

A well-groomed, middle-aged man in a clean, lemon and white baggy outfit walks on to the stage and bows to Lou, who returns the bow.

The dirge-like tune of 'Venus in Furs' strides triumphantly from the speakers. Gravelly low lyrics narrate the song's masochistic confessional. The band's cellist straddles her swaying instrument, sawing emphatically on her bow with one elbow, the other hand determining notes, her hair falling as over a pillow onto the source of an escalating, discordant, crescendo. With complete composure, the tai chi master enacts a soundless exercise in strength, grace, and poetry. We are witness to rock and roll as high art, New York style.

Lou contextualises once more. "The next song is going to feature Antony on vocals. We're a fan of his singing, and we've brought him out from our home town, New York, to be a part of this tour. When I first heard Antony sing, I knew he had the voice to do 'Candy Says' justice. My voice could never reach the notes that the song needed, but I think when you hear Antony sing it, you'll agree that he sings it beautifully."

The portly young man's voice quivers passionately as he expresses the lyric's worshipful tone.

How much of Lou Reed's music is unknown to me is attested with his homage to Edgar Allen Poe. *The Raven* album cover briefly appears before my inner eye, while the gravid emotion of Lou's oration takes thunderous possession. In an existential assertion of private will. With a ballistic conclusion of, "Never More!"

Antony's voice accompanies, singing, "For the new-found man."

When the house lights come on, bringing a false dawn, I can still hear the echo of the band's grand rambling and them singing, "For the new-found man."

47   River Deep, Mountain High

The decision to masturbate is justified. Once the idea has come into my head, there's no turning back. I have the single-bed room to myself in The Maze. From here on the pillow, two walls before me and the partly opened curtained windows looking across the building space onto opposite rooms, it feels like a private entitlement. There's a sense of having participated in the youthful tumbling across the way over-night. And a knowledge of there being a possibility of being seen but of not being seen now. The past is not important. I have a delivery to make. It is one way to start a birthday.

The Maze is a Nomads' backpackers. They have a camel as their symbol. It used to be called the CB Hotel and is at the bottom of Pitt Street around where The Pitt book and record shop used to be, down from Lawson's, and across the road from the People's Palace. "Harry" Burton used to be the night porter. He'd extended a gruff hand through the window grate to shake my hand once, but was mainly disinterested in the fact that we had known each other closely in the past. Harry had seen me on other occasions from that window but he had only extended the hand once. He had pounded heavily on my door at the end of one stay to let me know my time was up. In those *post-love* days he looked sickly and unpleasant, like an inhabitant of a bad dream. The place has changed a lot since converting from low-rent rooms to a backpackers' lodge. At reception, they have a choice of t-shirts with a maze design on them. I am tempted to select one from behind the friendly young staff at the new counter, yet decide against it.

On the train ride back home I foresee myself, down the rails, fronting for a massage later this afternoon. I can say to Michelle Brown as I enter Back to Health at 2pm, "I've just got off the train from Sydney."

Which I do when I arrive.

She has me lie on the table. A CD of whales in conference with a synthesizer calms the front room closed off from traffic on the Donald Street Bridge. Michelle, in her big and dumpy, light and heavy, curvy way, applies oil and pressure well into the tissues of my downcast neck and splayed legs. Her self-confident, operatic being assesses my bare back like an onlooking jury. My masseuse herself is subjected to a cross-examination. Her client (undercover) browsing porn at Nauti and Nice, had noticed her showing likeable discrimination in rejecting a pair of fluffy handcuffs presented to her by the ebullient sales assistant. With this in mind, since my introductory visit a month ago, my nudity under her pragmatic touch is excited by the possibility that she is a dominatrix. Even though Michelle has provided her modest background as a child singer in a girls' choir, a student at a local high school, and early motherhood with a Chilean guy, I cannot, for the duration of this sensual appointment, surrender the notion that she may have a drawer loaded with fetish toys. Each time she leaves the table to attend to another application, more oil or a CD to continue the consciousness, I half expect to be tied or teased with a leather aid.

Instead I pay a compliment. "You're a goddess!"

Michelle continues behind me with another operation, concealing, I suspect, a concessional smile.

I have flirted unsuccessfully. When turned over under a light sheet, the stiffness in my penis is beyond compromise. I can only feel a neglected pang as my masseuse tends dutifully to her scripted work and wordlessly overlooks the twitching head.

They are both slender young women. One occupies a couch in her skimpy underwear, the other, also undressed, addresses her firmly in Russian. She scolds her, spanks her, removes her panties from her tanned body and fingers her. A classical music soundtrack is interrupted at intervals by a recording of canned laughter. Observing from an armchair in my lounge-room, the porno video of lesbian coupling fixes my eyes and brings a warm flush of blood to my face. Under my clothing an instinctual animal is aroused, ready, and available.

I am indifferent to thoughts of modesty when knocking on my front door indicates Gerard and Tianshu's expected arrival. I welcome them in, fully aware that I am broadcasting an *interruptus* of sorts, that I smell. From a realm of secret recognition, I can see them sensing this with their eyes.

On our way to the Kent Hotel, we pass Gerard's old house at 86 Cleary Street.

He has moved on since then. "When Tianshu's parents saw the size of this place, they could not believe that it wasn't big enough for the two of us. They were shocked that we would be looking for something with more room. In China this would be a large house. Most people live in apartments."

Crossing Beaumont Street to the Kent, I see Bella from the Wetlands Green Corps team passing on the other side, her pronounced bottom in motion. I show her an open palm, she returns with a wave of her own, and a liquid-eyed smile. I take this as a favourable comment on the direction of my quickening desire.

Upon entering the Kent, Gerard, Tianshu and I find a table, and select meals from the bistro menu.

Each of the miniature bottles of port is enclosed in a light timber box. Gerard had explained to me that they came from Porto, which gives its name to port. The fortified wine was employed onboard sailing ships departing Portugal because its preservative nature kept it ripe for consumption after a long time at sea. One is white port, the other is red, each bottle is a souvenir from their overseas trip. I quickly try the first, finish it, and drink the second. The flavours mix sweetly as an aftertaste.

Unsure, I rehouse the porno video of the Russian lesbians anyway. Although a genuinely erotic film, and arthouse thanks to the strange soundtrack, I decide to surrender the disc for exchange. Not yet 10pm, I have time to return the tender love-making before Nauti and Nice closes. However, I remain uncertain whether this may be abandoning something of real value.

I am a regular at the shop, with respect to knowing my way around the shelves.

I come across a Dungeon Diaries package with red borders, four hours length and extra chapters, my fingers tighten on the plastic casing. A Rick Savage S&M production should adequately replace what I've left at the counter for exchange.

Homeward bound with a new sexy video, I have an expectant step for the promise of bounty carried in my bag.

This is a promise that often ends in disappointment. I am skipping through the scenes, surpassing thresholds of steepness advising closure with an appetite for more, a gambling zeal ultimately culminating in obsession and failure.

It only takes a single glitch, whether it be poor surface quality on a disrespected disc or indifferent content, to make me overwhelmed and overdosed.

Keith drives the car onto the footpath in front of the Red Shield store.

We carry the large brown armchair onto the street and lower it to the pavement while Keith raises the back door. There's enough room inside the station-wagon to take the lounge lying on one side. The ache in my twisted back remains after last night's marathon, however there's some consolation in this morning's pledge to replace the offending chair with a more comfortable one. When Keith returns me and the new second-hand lounge to Oliver Street, I express gratitude for his help but I am left doubting whether this 30-dollar purchase really guarantees a better future.

48   Short People

Earlier, I had told Stacey Ross my old primary school was having a 50th anniversary and I was thinking of going.

Her path and mine often crossed at the Wetlands Centre. She had made a strong first impression, rather feisty, certain in what she wanted, sure of her ability to take on tasks. She walked with a bob, like the upright strut of a Scottish dancer, had thick wavy hair tied in a pony-tail, lucid light blue eyes, a touch of freckles, and a prominent bottom. I can remember her telling me about going to see David Bowie on his *Reality* tour, wearing a revealingly short dress, which was okay as long as she didn't bend over! Stacey told me things about herself that were surprisingly confessional, a trait, as she later described, of her over-sharing. When I told her about Eleebana Public School's coming 50th anniversary, she was busy setting up a children's birthday party.

"Do you think you'll go?"

"Well, I am thinking about it. It would be good to catch up with some of the people from Eleebana."

But I didn't. I went to a yoga class instead.

The rear window of Ashtanga Yoga looks onto the derelict shell of the Jolly Roger nightclub, the ghost dance floor and the empty bar.

On the mat all my cares are exercised away. With a series of positions, firstly standing, followed by sitting, then stretching and up-ending, all performed in counts of five breaths, or twenty for the final shoulder stand, I can feel my body respond to an ancient healing ritual.

Afterwards, I enjoy a sensation of improved posture as I walk along King Street into town.

In the Hunter Street mall, on a well-placed public seat, I drink a freshly-stirred, toxin-cleansing fruit juice, bought from a cubicle outside David Jones.

Chris and Elizabeth appear and approach me, showing their usual keenness for my company. Today we are in the outer world, apart from our usual context at the Wetlands Centre. This seems to invest our unplanned meeting with a heightened sense of opportunity. That today is also my birthday gives us further reason to indulge each other. From my seat I tell them about seeing *Kung Fu Hustle* last night at the Showcase. The cinema's distinctive facade occupies the streetscape opposite us.

"It is a very funny film."

Chris and Liz agree, Chris relates they have seen it reviewed on *At The Movies*.

As it is lunch-time I accept their offer to eat at the Subway outlet a block further down the mall.

At an inside table we devour six-inch rolls that have been prepared by the latex-gloved hands of an employed sandwich artist.

Then, we continue to the Great Northern Hotel.

The inside of the pub has been renovated, giving the front bar a spacious feel. The three of us carry our drinks to a table in a side area. Liz does not drink anything alcoholic because of her medication for epilepsy, while Chris and I satisfy ourselves with beers. He talks at length about a series they have been watching on Egyptology.

"They had made so many discoveries... they knew exactly where to put the opening so that the sun would shine in... all of these things came from the Egyptians."

He speaks with genuine admiration, as if the programmes have raised his consciousness. I think to myself, what is the purpose of knowing these things? Yet I also acknowledge the cultural inebriation Chris experiences has its own value. If only as an interesting topic for conversation within a hotel's architecture.

His subject matter does seem oddly out of place here. But it gives his intellect a cause and transcends the sheltered lives he and Liz share in their Mayfield abode, one removed from the grand interior design of the Great Northern. This needful disregard for pretence gives Chris an endearing outsider trait. I feel an authentic tie of friendship towards him.

As we part ways, and I thank them both for helping me to celebrate my birthday, Chris and Liz reply that they are equally pleased to have been involved. Once more I am struck with a feeling of abiding friendship towards Chris. However, a secondary awareness, that this is a burgeoning sentiment yet to evolve, also dawns on me.

Neither Gerard nor Keith are available this Friday afternoon, so as a way of keeping the birthday spirit alive I phone Franca at home. Since volunteering at the Wetlands she has become an enthusiastic companion.

"Hello, it's you!"

Franca has much to talk about from her condominium kitchen in Merewether. Our conversation begins to consume time more profoundly than telephone handsets can accommodate. Verbal intercourse itself has become an ordeal. The changing of hands holding the receiver to relieve tiredness, soreness in the primary listening ear, and thoughts preoccupied with seeking a polite way to terminate the call are all signals the telephone conversation is overly long.

"Enjoy what's left of your birthday, Geoff."

I follow Franca's conclusion by promptly sliding a Van Morrison CD into my trusty, royal-blue Sony ghetto-blaster. A familiar and companionable sound lifts my confused and disappointed thoughts while dinner cooks, and what's left of the evening ensues.

I have been recording episodes of Martin Scorsese's *The Blues* on my programmable NEC VHS player. The episode that I watch tonight, after retiring to the lounge-room with its cheap, just sufficient, chandelier lighting, is one titled *Piano Blues*. Archival footage shifts between dextrous musicians running expressive fingers up and down keyboards in an array of notes while Scorsese in the background adds his adoring commentary. I lose track of who the featured artists are. An incessant piano music accompanies me to bed, and permeates my being.

49 Layla

How accepted and included I feel as the girls at reception sing 'Happy Birthday to You' in cheerful unison. Lee, slender, dedicated, and Linda, shapely, spirited, greet me at the front desk with a cake, a single flickering candle, and a generous little ceremony.

"I am being serenaded by angels."

With further grace, they supply a large slice of rich cake on a plate to accompany my lunch. My mouth, extended with emotion, consumes so much that when I return to work on this slow Saturday at the Wetlands, I carry the extra weight of having eaten too much.

After work, the celebration continues with an introduction to Bob Dylan's new *Modern Times* album. It has a sturdy compressed cardboard sleeve that fits over the two recordings like a durable book cover. I notice the bonus disc is a DVD of film clips made of the songs.

Even though an almighty thunderstorm has begun smashing from above, I take a leap of faith, based on claims made by surge boards and adaptors, to keep all media plugged in and playable. But I do remove the receiver from the phone as a precaution.

Dylan appears on the screen like a preserved Southern gentleman. He intones astride a microphone, dressed like his reverent band in the style of a horseman on a special mission. His, and their, loyalty to an old worldly muse defies any present threat posed as the storm gate-crashes all around.

The audio CD launches with a challenge to the tempest.

"There's thunder on the mountain..."

The album's stomping rockabilly opener brakes for a slow, backwoods number, picks up again for an up-tempo blues, steps down for a country romance, then spins through tracks in turns wishful and resigned, archaic, prophetic, and stridently proud.

"The levee's gonna break..."

The rain drowns out the sound.

I've been under the spell of Dylan and the band's worldview for about an hour. It is a grand commentary that draws on a time befitting and suiting the modern world, because it is so not of it. I have enjoyed the album greatly.

When I check for expected birthday messages on my phone, I discover that Mum has tried a few times, eventually bemoaning that I am a hard man to reach!

Her voice has become touchingly distinct ever since a mysterious affliction has affected her ability to breathe and orate.

When we finally speak she maintains, "You need another CD like a hole in the head."

And with this sentiment as my only company, today's feat is stilled to a mood of sated familiarity.

Thanks Mum.

50   Nobody's Fault but Mine

I am bopping. Abe has recognised me in the dance crowd. He looms over me for a moment with his Elvis-like sideburns and hair, and remarks with drunken excitement on the coincidence of us dancing together to Ash Grunwald's blues here at Bimbadgen. This has made his day. And it has made mine too.

Gemma is jiving in the crowd. We are brother and sister doing our thing on this early September Saturday afternoon in the Hunter Valley.

Before this de-stressing dance our day has included a long and drawn-out coach trip starting at the bus depot next to Newcastle Station, via a queued ladies' toilet stop at a park in Weston, and onward to the extensive carparks of Bimbadgen Estate, vineyard and venue for today's Red, White and Blues Festival.

Gemma is accompanying me for my fiftieth birthday. She arrived yesterday evening, after catching a train down from her hometown of Bellingen.

A smaller venue on the hill catches our attention. The Fumes on drums and guitar are playing their manic two-man blues, ladies and children just out of prams are dancing to the grooves of the Extended Family band, and Dallas Frasca with her slide and vocals brings her gentleman guitarist nearly to his knees.

Gemma and I unfold our chairs. From the steep slope we look down on the main stage and out to the vast water-coloured hills. The two of us take in the view. In the lake of similar-aged punters, I see a familiar face.

We hear Chain, who play an expected set-list.

"I can remember when I was young."

We see The Backsliders. They have changed their line-up, with Rob Hirst now drumming loudly, Ian Collard on harmonica and only Dom Turner keeping them sounding like they used to with his plaintive Aussie vocals and slide-guitar.

I make my way down the hill, around bigger groups of people and couples, to reach the flatter area in front of the stage where the bands are not so loud. Then climb back up the hill to Gemma energised by the music.

Sunday morning a week later is the true day of my birthday. But the day rings false without any phone call from Mum. Her death last year has taken her voice away from us. I face today as another day of readying myself to go to a job that must be done.

When I enter the Visitors Centre the ladies at the front desk surprise me with not one, but two bottles of red. From Lee there's a merlot and from Linda a cabernet-shiraz.

The news of my 50th has spread to the members of Technophobe, the Centre's lunchtime entertainment. As I sit on the stage with Linda sharing lunch, Phil acknowledges my birthday by dedicating their folk-jazz version of 'Sunday Morning Coming Down' to me.

Throughout the afternoon I am buoyed by the attention, and the lonely sentiments conveyed by the lyrics of this stirring country song.

"There's something in a Sunday that makes a body feel alone..."

The train home from work pulls into Hamilton Station. The walk to the Kent is a well-worn path. The relaxed afternoon air offers little resistance as I encounter the subdued pace of a Beaumont Street Sunday afternoon ebbing towards evening.

Through the swing doors the front bar greets me with low light and a careful clinking of glass. My attention turns to Gerard and Tianshu, perched at a side table by the window. Gerard offers his hand to shake mine firmly.

"Happy 50th Geoff."

Tianshu says the same, so I give her my hand to shake softly.

Soon after Keith enters from the front door. He peers for a moment into the indoor setting, and then approaches us with a slightly self-conscious tilt. I become aware that Keith and Gerard as friends have separate relationships and know each other only vaguely. I find this disorientating, as if my identity is incomplete.

We take a seat at a bench table in the beer garden. Gerard announces I can order whatever I want from the menu as they will be shouting. I sense Keith may be tentative about Gerard's magnanimity. But I reckon to myself they can afford it.

"I think I'll have the barramundi, thanks."

Gerard supports my decision. The others tend toward steaks. We eat well and our conversation agrees, however Keith does not stay much longer than the duration of his meal.

With our departure sometime later, I notice the familiar countenance of Jeff Whaley sitting at a table in the front bar. Always voluble, he greets us with his remnant London accent.

"What brings you to the Kent on this Sunday evening?"

I explain the occasion. So Jeff, coincidentally met, wishes me a heartfelt Happy 50th.

A pastel-coloured cooler bag sits on my front doorstep. The pleasant surprise of an unexpected gift conflicts with a suspicion of theft, as both involve a trespass.

In the better-light of my kitchen, I am able to read the note which explains the little mystery. It is written by a cousin who I don't often see. She was visiting a friend in Hamilton and, thanks to intra-family knowledge, has dropped by to deliver this humble package at my address. I sense this gesture filling, in its modest way, the gap that's understood to be left by Mum's death. The cooler bag contains an assortment of edible produce, along with Sheila's hand-written birthday wish also from *Angus, Declan, Tyrone, Robbie, and baby Liam.* Their thoughtful gift emits a discreet radiant light, like that which emanates from a jewellery box. For a moment I soak it up.

Although we are having dinner together a week after, I tell Franca I have sought her company because of a requirement to celebrate my 50th with *all* of my friends. She seems to take this admission with some amount of offence.

Our attendance at Sticky Rice, downstairs in the renovated Crown and Anchor hotel, is due to Franca's recommendation of the tasty Thai menu. I am uncomfortably aware that her usual ebullience is somehow subdued, as if something about me is bothering her. Once more, I wonder whether having a relationship based on mere familiarity, without any development of intimacy, is such a good idea.

I tell Franca about the coincidence of Gerard giving me the same series of *Countdown Wonder Years* that she had troubled to copy, adding that these discs lacked the defect qualities of her CDs as well as included two DVDs of film clips. She seems displeased to hear that her cottage industry effort has been upstaged by a better product.

After our meals, we discuss Dad and Marg travelling overseas together and how we are encouraged to witness the support they are giving each other. Franca states her belief that they should become romantically attached. I cannot agree with her proposition while she in turn remains adamant about the veracity of her view. I guess my resistance is because I'm still grieving Mum and thus unwilling to see Dad coupled with Marg, but the explanation I give Franca is more directive.

"They would not think that way about it."

51   It Started with a Kiss

ENGL2202 PORTFOLIO   *Geoffrey Nicholls 2008*
FIFTY-FIRST SOLILOQUY

I have a sudden sensation, soon after waking, that this day is special, as if my worth is valued from another view or a different head occupies my flattened pillow. An androgynous herald has the sole purpose of informing me today is my 51st birthday. A momentary embrace accompanies the message before spreading across my bed like an open door.

My morning walk is wrapped in joy, it flows through me yet exercises restraint. Tranquility, I have learned, is just enough. The sunlit surfaces keep equilibrium with my measured steps. The key for today, I know, does not belong to me. An attractive woman jogs past with a cheerful exchange.

The car stops with no indication of turning, the roads are not busy now and there is time to wait. Sometimes motorists neglect to communicate a turn, this vehicle blinkers late. My sarcasm grows with an urge to protest. Virgos are influenced by Mars, and I know this means war. Only last century, the tidy numerology of the ninth of the ninth, nineteen ninety-nine was upset by conflict. While East Timor hacked itself to pieces, I jettisoned civility with Dad and close friends to take a stand. Directing punches at a phantom driver just goes with the territory.

I live a structured life. The Shortland Wetlands has been my employer for 20 years. Outside that part-time work, I have a private gardening job on Fridays, study literature at the University of Newcastle, attend choir rehearsals on Tuesday nights and gentle yoga classes on Wednesday mornings. My social life tends to follow this pattern of organisation. On occasion, there is variation, as there is today. I text Janet to let her know I need to substitute gardening with writing a critical essay.

"That's okay and enjoy your birthday," she replies.

I am surprised. "You remembered?"

"Of course!" she returns, with the trill of an ensconced bird.

There is one call that cannot be heard today, the sound of a mother's voice orientating all birthdays to unconditional love.

It is surreal to be saluted when you live alone. Sporadic moments of attention encounter intervals of strange disquiet. The act of sorting clothes into a wash-basket becomes an animated dance between longing and belonging. I am loading the tub when my reflection in the bathroom mirror, in an expression of triumph and doubt, looks back.

"A snarl in the smile, a seed in the marmalade!"

A dear, older friend is dying. I lapse into a state of deep pledging, soothed by the lullabies of the blind Aboriginal singer, Gurrumul, but I sink too deep and become entangled in pitying emotion.

Something happens when my spiritual well fills, an urge to share erupts, placing an implosive stress on its walls. I search my heart for a language that mends.

The full clothesline looks regal as it dries, ushered on by a clear breeze. My essay notes on "Rain" lie gathered in the shadows of a plan. Midday rests poised on a precious coin, vivid self-portraiture on one side and invisibility on the next. I am compelled to make a phone call to an absent friend, to simply celebrate that I exist. I clutch the handset with both hands, they are like pioneers on a mission that could change a river's course. Our conversation peels open emptily. My sovereign need exhibits itself before an indifferent crowd, their evasive terms draw a dull curtain across my attempt. Hanging up, I am left gaping toward a foreign outline. Essay ideas are wire rope, and washing may rot where it is pegged.

The afternoon passes in combat between inclusion and rejection. Tenacity, in an umpire's role, guides me through each undecided round. I apply myself to disillusionment until Gerard arrives at five o'clock. We have a mutual recognition of our birthdays, his being on the fifth and mine on the ninth of September. The door is open to my guest with a firm handshake and a jet-lagged forbearance. Two grown men stand to unwrap their gifts, brown tissue paper reveals tokens as sincere as our valued friendship. Two beers are raised, as the harsh afternoon sunbeams become a mellower light. Promises are made that may be broken, yet our intentions keep a common pact. The space left by Gerard at six is occupied by a small wooden figure of a moose. Decorated with the Norwegian flag it hoists a silver paper clamp like a spear.

Tuesday is also singing night. The upstairs room in Hamilton draws me out with the social suck of a magnet. Our torsos in harmony do not test for opposites. That today was soured is soon lost in sweet chords and amusement.

Fresh, nocturnal air nourishes these half a century old lungs. Cooler temperatures locate restive beverages in this weak bladder. I manage the last block home with a furtive stride. In backyard darkness, my fingers negotiate a liberating stream, at the same time a soft, unwelcome pad adheres beneath a shoe. My faculties work to remove the spell left by the Devil or a local mutt. I reach the tap in hops, and balance there, raising my foot. The shit clings to a short-lived victory. I employ surgical strokes of a stick and an old toothbrush to erase the brown gloat. The upturned sole adopts a rubbery grin, then sings.

"Happy birthday to you, happy birthday to you, happy birthday dear Geoffrey, happy birthday to you!"

52   I'll Be Your Mirror

We have the room to ourselves, but we usually have to rearrange the tables and chairs to create an open space. The aim is to get the tables on the window side facing those along the entrance wall and some faced towards the front of the room where Ed positions himself. The arrangement does not always have a neat result, as there are often students seated in the way and askew.

The classroom on the first floor of the Social Sciences building has a door to the left of where the stairs reach the main waiting area. We enter the room as students enrolled in Advanced Creative Writing's second semester. I arrive today with the usual compulsions of high expectation and quiet disappointment and orientate my table toward the students opposite, the door, and Ed's punctual entrance.

Today we are studying selected paragraphs from Junot Diaz's cross-cultural *Drown*. Ed begins with a close reading of the text that soon involves him giving a translation for the Hispanic word "pato", meaning gay. In this typical manner, he guides us through the language and themes in our weekly topical readings. The short story *Drown* describes tensions felt by an ethnic minority Spanish-American teenager. The author frequently references Spanish terms, an uncompromising tool, rendering the text not easily accessible to non-Hispanic readers.

A scene in a swimming pool containing elements of trespass, sexuality, and even juvenile delinquency, connects *Drown* with *Greasy Lake,* a text we studied in one of Keri's classes. Keri then stated a personal interest in the story due to her own Wagga teenage years when locations on darker margins were sought for risk-taking fun. While one fellow student has commented on this tendency as an indication of her being weird, Ed has forthrightly defended Keri's integrity.

"She is a colleague and a friend."

Ed's, and our, study of *Drown* concludes that the narrator is unable to escape the hold of his neighbourhood. He is estranged from his friend, who has gained a ruthless freedom for himself, and appears to be drowning in the blue television glow of his mother's self-pity.

Yet it can be asked, does his duty to his mother symbolise an important life-role inadvertently found?

Lionel's workshop paper, on the desk before me, keeps attentively to the cross-cultural theme. I briefly inspect his face to see evidence of his Japanese heritage. He does have a slightly Asiatic complexion and demeanour, although it is scarcely defined by his looks. This is a sensitive piece. I find the capitalisation of all personal pronouns in his writing disconcerting and begin circling them and correcting, to upper-case, lower-case first letters which have been overlooked, but by the fourth paragraph I stop. The content of Lionel's short story takes precedence. How he was instructed in tea ceremony by his grandmother. I contribute just a few grammar and punctuation notes to the printed sheet. Followed by a decisive tick for the penultimate paragraph.

In his commentary, Lionel expresses the significance of the ritual to his true identity.

Jenny Carroll's cultural subject comes from the Hunter coalfields. Under the title of *Victim*, Jenny's short story is a portrait of gamely crude teenage individualism. The narrator is compromised and eventually degraded by her and her friend Christine's lack of inhibition and promiscuous rebellion. One morning, she awakes barely dressed and defiled in a park to discover Christine has abandoned her in the night to be exploited. This unsavoury immersion has made her determined to remove her self-demeaning ways, and undermining friend, from her life.

From a desk next to her boyfriend, Jenny maintains a confident distance between herself and the protagonist in her story.

Her hair hangs like a King Charles wig, or a spaniel's ears, down either side of her emergent face. Lucy always has a goofy alertness about her, as if she were from another era when young women were dolefully obedient. She told me once that she was doing a double degree, both in Arts and Education. When as first-year English students we had this discussion, Lucy professed an adherence to Classics as her favourite subject.

3078943 Lucy Braithwaite's paper is titled *Canis*. "Which means dog."

As she reads her writing out loud, Lucy's upright torso leans a little forward over the desk and the pages laid in front of her. Her words sound at home in the context of Ancient Rome and the plight of a young male slave. Lucy's narrative seems to inhabit a plot and characterisation from a time already lived and documented, her careful reading a service of translation.

From across the room, I compliment Lucy on her ability to speak from a male's point of view. Her eyes widen.

53   The Carnival is Over

I start the day across the O'Connell Bridge, on the other side of the Liffey. After rising with an itchy sensation due to sleeping in underpants dampened by the gyrating buttocks of a lap dancer on a foolhardy night in Temple Bar, I buy a fruit juice alongside a worldly woman making her morning purchase in a small supermarket opposite the river. I am then given a helping hand by staff at Tourist Information with directions to a travel agent on Abbey Street. This takes me to an Eircom public phone.

"Hello Gemma, it's Geoffrey. I just thought I'd let you wish me happy birthday."

"Geoffrey!"

We chat for a while, the phone card maintaining credit throughout the call. Gemma comments that I have picked up an Irish accent. I speak naturally to my sister about how I am travelling, and think to myself, this helps.

I find the travel agent on Abbey Street. A familiar consultant deftly complies, making a booking on the ferry from Dun Laoghaire to Holyhead. I make my way to the Luas stop and wait there until boarding a light rail to The Point, where I hope to locate the Dublin ferry terminal.

I cannot explain why I walk alone in the vacuum of the Dublin docks with my fly unzipped, my genitals breathing in the air and peering shyly out.

A woman roller skates by and I follow her lead, crossing the road without checking for traffic. I become distraught. I am an occupant in a world that is open and grey, the road, the warehouses, the railway and fences, an embodiment of emptiness. My reason for being here is to sight the Dublin ferry terminal, but it is nowhere to be found. The reality of the docks is too vast.

A train travels through the scene, the drivers seem to be caught in a meaningless momentum. I check my fly.

A sculpture of three wolves in a pack stands under a Ferris wheel at The Point. They do not look friendly. A foursome of European tourists are assembled in their vicinity, and to me they represent all of humanity. They ask me if I will take a photo of them and when they pose for photographs by the wheel, I cannot help noticing the breasts on the only woman. I wonder, returning their camera, whether they will like what I took for them.

A Luas carries me away from The Point, now known as the O2 arena. Away from the memory of a Christy Moore concert captured on CD, somewhere far more communal and humble than the current venue. Away from the Dublin docks and their non-existent ferries. Returning me to the heart of the city on O'Connell Street.

Back in O'Connell Street, I re-locate the library to use my newly registered card to book time on the internet. To pass the queuing time, I scan the newspaper classifieds for sex clubs and, with more sense, a book on Jack Yates' life and art. I peruse photographs of Derry that appear, with apology, to be rather corny. When a computer becomes free a Polish lady is sitting beside me. She is chatting with a friend and, although she is a mum with a young daughter close by, she has a sexy allure. The conversation is hushed, yet an older man still has to ask them to quieten down.

Over lunch in a café next door to O'Brien's, I make a mental note to acknowledge that I am desperate. On a corner to a market lane, I notice an amateurish sign saying IRISH FORTUNE-TELLERS. An old man points me in the direction of a stairway.

There are two women upstairs, Maria and Laura (I think) are seated. On tables lie packets of cigarettes and cards. It is like a cheap hairdressers'. For the cost of twenty Euros, I receive from the unhealthy-looking older of the two, a card and hand reading only.

"You will meet someone and not be alone when you die, a tall blonde woman in your circle of friends is interested, three children but may not be yours, start a business the opportunity is current, long life and good love, some anger that you keep to yourself in your left thumb... "

The cards she reads have flowers prints, I am not interested in the flowers.

"You are hard to get close to, you need to open up more, you have important decisions to make, but you have a good head on your shoulders and will make the right decision."

She goes on to say that I don't trust everything she says. Then she asks do I have anything else I would like to know? My mind goes blank. The other woman, (Maria or Laura, I'm not sure), notices this pause and announces, "You're blank... You'll go blind." I cannot be certain which.

"You will receive a letter in the next fortnight that will disappoint, but must be overcome, will be on medication, but not to worry, only antibiotics, and will visit a hospital for someone else early next year."

The three of us make small talk. The other elderly woman, (who may be the reader's sister), speaks about Australian Aborigines, remarking on the fact that they have their own police. Then, in unison, they wish me well.

All is well, except, I may be blind... it's not certain. Biddies, I think to call them, rip-off merchants too.

Two women are sleeping in our dorm. After having a shower, I entertain remaining in only my underpants while I fossick in my bag for a while, but this lewd notion is tempered by a young man's sudden entrance to the room. The interruption is for the best as in place of my exhibition a conversation arises. This is mostly with the awakened librarian from Washington D.C. We talk about the library of the Linen Hall in Belfast, the one with the creaking floors and polished timber. I discover that the Dewey Decimal System has been replaced by the Library of Congress alphabetical system.

"The Qs are science."

I believe that Chaplain's, across the road from the Screen Cinema off Temple Bar, because of its modest size, embodies the worth of an Irish pub entirely. Although customers do mingle, a respectful quietness is maintained, allowing one to enjoy a half-pint of Guinness in peace.

The big guy with tatts and a wound on his head is manning the box office at the Screen Cinema as he also was last night when I enquired about *Black Dynamite*. He recognises me as I buy a ticket for *His and Hers*.

Before the film, I must spend time orientating myself on the upward-looking seat.

His and Hers is a documentary with a subdued, naturalistic tone. It provides women from the Irish Midlands, from where last night's lap dancer hails, the opportunity to discuss the males in their lives, be they father, boyfriend, husband, son, or no-one. Only the female points of view are given, children, teenagers, young adults, mid-adults, mature, or elderly women, all talking about men. This is something males might find boring, as I do, yet real enough.

A beer in a crowded corner hotel in Temple Bar helps me drown some sorrow. I listen to songs being belted out by a male in a ponytail, such sing-alongs as Colin Hay's 'Who Can It Be Now?', Dylan and Van Morrison, and all to good effect. Here to the side of the room, I experience a moment of timelessness. I'm in thrall of a woman keeping company. She is quintessentially Irish. Her eyes dig into mine as she speaks in voracious gestures with a friend. In seeing her, I understand the command of a woman's need. I am sorry to have to leave tomorrow. Her and Ireland.

In the bustling street by the plaza, I encounter a stocky young man wearing green baggy tracksuit pants and a dullard's haircut. His unruly, grocer's assistant's, lack of style is overruled by his triumphantly angelic renditions of sentimental pop favourites that tug at my core. He keeps time with a gentle man strumming guitar by his side. They have CDs for sale. But I wonder whether the repertoire may be too safe. I figure I could hear him from the dining-room on the first floor of the Quay Hotel, so I go up there to listen and deliberate.

My arrival upstairs brings me to a nearly empty land where the gasps of music from the world outside have become cushioned to silence by the steps and the heavy timber balustrades and then the dining-room floor.

The quiet interior is familiar to me, as this is my third time here. First, I came with Gerard and Tianshu at the end of a long day exploring the tourist sites of Dublin. Next, Gerard and I met alone after his work at Trinity College and my visit to the Irish National Gallery where I found Jack Yate's sublime *After the Rain*. We had enjoyed ourselves, as much as in old times with an Irish stew and Guinness. The waitress tonight is the same Chinese. Slender and tall, radiant and astute, her friendly descant reminds me of the times spent here before.

I am still at repast when the waitress returns, stands close to my table and speaks. I am consumed by an urge to touch her pubic mound, but in truth I am barely able to negotiate the notion of crossing the gulf to her nearer hip. Besotted with indecision, everything around me converts to a charade as I sort through the Euros to pay my bill.

The waitress stands in the night air outside the Quay. For a while she lets me hold her hand.

"I cannot understand being single, you need to have someone to share things with, true things that matter to you."

She knows in herself she will get married and have a child when she goes back to China.

"Maybe it's because I'm Chinese."

There are Spanish talkers, French talkers, and Italian talkers, a cacophony of talkers, all reporting loudly in Abigail's common-room. I let myself be overwhelmed and overlooked because I need to experience the rest of the day not alone. Their different demographic means a level of alienation is to be expected. With no more than commonplace self-pity, I uproot myself from the animated din and privately mount the stairs, knowingly following the trails of two voluptuous females.

At my floor, I sit for a few moments on the red-carpeted steps and reflect. A nice young woman with sun-tanned breasts passes by. A young French man stops and asks me if I am alright.

The French man is from our room, he and Michael, the polite German guy, are engaged in thoughtful conversation from their top bunks. Of the other occupants, it is the red-haired of the two ladies who speaks with me this time. She tells me about an ordeal she has had to endure. An Irish man had rubbed her arse and told her she had good breasts. From the partial concealment of her lower bunk, her librarian friend, on the other hand, keeps quiet about their night.

In time, I turn off the lights on behalf of all five.

With a whispered, "Thanks."

54   Fox Hunter

Fridays, when Leather Feather comes to town to play at the Lass O'Gowrie, now have a new direction and a sense of purpose. The catalyst is Steve Evans, who makes the trip up from Sydney with a head full of music. When he, oddly hunched in an open-necked shirt, dress hat and jacket, fronts the band and uses his forced mellow voice, or turns sideways to the amplifier to dominate his guitar, he is ably joined by his lanky brother Chris on bass, Dale seated at drums, and Pucko, a stalwart of local bands, lending a hand on rhythm guitar. The Leather Feather gigs of grungy pop and psychedelia have become occasions for loyal, older punters to gather together. I have this in mind as I control the vacuum cleaner around furniture edges at home, a Nick Lowe vocal just audible above the unhealthy roar of the outdated Electrolux. As I dust over bookcases, and fall into a kinky maid mode of thought, I anticipate the likelihood of the sexy Lingard sisters being there tonight and wonder whether role-playing as a housewife may make me not manly enough for them. I am already noting the coolness of listening to the Nick Lowe anthology as a depicted birthday activity.

Reunions at the Lass have been happening on a regular two-monthly basis. On the Friday night in July, I was surprised to see Allen Doncaster moving from the bar. He met my startled look with less surprise, his "Hallo Nic" being followed with a gesture akin to returning a book to a shelf.

I can remember the discussion later on, as our numbers grew around tables under cover in the beer garden, about the ethos borne by punk rock. In particular, the movement's arrogance. With swilling eyes, Don piping up, "I think that arrogance was good."

And later again, languidly inebriated and backed by an external wall, Don declaring after another puff, "All people are horrible, Nic." Spoken with conviction, his assertion made me aware I had come far from holding such views.

Besides embodying a buried past, there was a further, speculative, dimension to Don's reappearance. In recent years, I have been having a recurring dream of us sharing the occupancy of a multi-storied boarding house. He had an appointed room, ensconced in the building, whereas my place seemed to fluctuate from a downstairs apartment with a landing to approaches at the front of the building, in door-ways, on stairs, along corridors, or in meetings with fellow tenants in dubious abodes and threatened by dislocation. Throughout these boarding-house dreams Don's presence remained a constant. Which had made me wonder, as I knew Don was living and working in London and was unlikely to reside in Newcastle again.

By way of explanation, he had returned to look after his dad. But now, he told me, he held the "dubious honour" of having, "run away from my father," and was living in Whitebridge, which he described in terms of "absolute inertia."

The anticipation of running into Don has since become a feature of the Friday night Leather Feather gigs and, sure enough, he is here. Soon after meeting, he dips into his coat pocket and presents to me a handful of CDs wrapped in paper folders.

"These are mainly West African recordings, although I've put in some from Ethiopia, too. They play incredible music. They're heavily influenced by western jazz... at times, it's as if you are in a dance hall in the colonial 1930s, you can see the pillars and the palms, the men in their suits... I don't know where they get it from. The *Pirates Choice* album was really popular... had quite a following in London when it came out."

He shows me the neatly hand-written labels, and when I recognise Ali Farka Toure's name, Don exclaims how pure and elemental his music is. I am touched by the sentiment expressed in the sharing of this handful of treasured sources.

When the music starts, Don moves nearer to the band. With his head leaned forward, and a beer held in his hand, he stands close enough to cheer remarks as they play.

Rhonda is another usual suspect, an old acquaintance rediscovered on these valued Friday nights. Appearing through the clouds of denial that have obscured us from keeping in touch since she and Rick parted and she moved down here, Rhonda has also exposed a need to re-belong whenever Leather Feather brings it on. Like a hand sliding into a trusted glove, my sister-in-law merges back in with the crowd.

Rhonda has an endearing trait of remaining faithful to occasions such as Christmas and birthdays, and in the beer garden tonight, she takes a book from her bag and hands it to me.

"Happy birthday Geoff."

She informs me the book is by the author of the spooky movie *Never Let Me Go* and that he also wrote *The Remains of the Day*. She is surprised that he is Japanese yet writes such quintessentially English stories.

I thank her, and securing the edition in my backpack, I notice the fresh detail and newness of its cover.

"Happy Birthday, Nic."

Brimful with cheer and her eyes soft with goodwill, Justine addresses me from a place true to herself, steeped in kindness. It borders on unconditional love, or maybe she's just friendly. Anyhow, I love her warm hug.

Extracting myself from these heartbeats of embrace, I stake a path through the pub and the punters in a conscious effort of premature departure. As I cordially unlink from friends and fortunes, I internally counsel.

You need to make your farewells... in order to leave early... when you have a working day looming the next morning.

Anyway, I'm feeling tired.

Met with the night air in Railway Street, as I make a solitary crossing over the silent railway line, a notion occurs, holds, then lessens. To the sound of laughter, I am made aware that I had no headway into her sparkling amber web tonight. The thought of the younger Lingard sister stalls me, for a moment, before the long walk home.

"I'm sorry I missed your birthday. Let me know when it arrives."

Stacey Ross's gift comes in the mail a few weeks later. The cause for the delay is explained when I see the postcode that has been written incorrectly and then corrected by a postal worker. Inside the neatly addressed package, I discover both a postcard and a paperback.

The book, with the title *Demian,* is by Hermann Hesse. I am thrilled as he has been a favourite author. The all-black cover features only a mysterious orange globe, some white geometric font, and a prominent sticker, "Winner of the Nobel Prize in Literature". The slender volume exudes significance.

Stacey's postcard portrays, in muted washed tones, a collage-like painting of a crowd assembled in a German plaza. A busy and articulated formal scene. I read the back of the card.

2011.   *Dear Geoff,*   ☺ *(HAPPY BIRTHDAY)* ☺
Happy 54th Birthday! Hope you have a wonderful day ☺
Thanks for the years of friendship & look forward to many more.
I saw 'The Mad Square – Modernity in German Art' exhibition
today & thought you would enjoy it ☺ *I got the book & card there.*
I hope you haven't read the book (I haven't – but it looked good
and suited to you!) I liked this card as I have been there. The card
depicts the artists in the square trying to convince the powers that
be that their art is worthwhile! ENJOY/ 'STACEY'/ XO

I open the book to the inside cover.

2011.

Dear Geoff,

Happy 54th Birthday!

Have a wonderful day and I hope you enjoy Demian *an ideas*
book for an ideas man ☺

Enjoy the selfhood journey in Demian *& your own continuing*
journey!

Stacey xo

Stacey's lasting and expanding recognition of me as a friend
keeps me intrigued about the prospect of a future relationship.

I know there is the age difference. And there's that social
intelligence she has gained from her school-teaching, church,
and sundry friends in Sydney and overseas. And her travels.
But she has such an influence over me when she shares so
over-sharingly.

With care, I place the book with its card on a shelf. Pledged
to be read as soon as possible.

55 (This Must Be the Place) Naïve Melody

My mountain bike is called "Kevin", after Kevin Rudd's stimulus package in 2009. I used the government's $900 to buy it and a new monitor for my computer. The bike is a Giant, grey-black and white, with a solid frame. I find Kevin a little heavy to lift, but the weight also argues durability. When I went overseas on long-service leave, I left it locked under the back veranda covered over with a sheet of black plastic. During the time I was away in Ireland, the wind or the builders must have lifted, or left, the sheet off the bike, because rust has formed on the front forks and fittings. Otherwise, it's still in good condition, and would probably be like new if it had been stored indoors. These days, Kevin is kept in the shed that takes up most of the backyard.

I slide up the roller-door. There's a lot of room inside. I perform the task of removal with an arc-like movement. After closing the roller-door, I wheel Kevin up the path between the fence and the side of the house to the driveway. Here I mount the bike and, propelled by the concrete slope of the drive across the gutter, arrive on the raised bitumen surface of Oliver Street. I enjoy the vigour in my legs as the wheels turn and my journey begins for real.

A brisk momentum must soon be slowed to a coast, and then a light brake, as I look for cars turning into Cleary from Samdon, or driving down Cleary from Beaumont, before I make a careful left turn out, followed by a right turn into Swan, another right onto Lindsay, and then a left into Steel.

While I have the great crowns of the Moreton Bay figs in Gregson Park hovering above my right shoulder, my left shrugs past the Seventh Day Adventist church, and continues shirking from crouched car doors until after the Greek Orthodox church, with its baleful Sunday chanting. Both shoulders then open for a fast pedal to meet the traffic lights ahead.

At Glebe Road, I dismount and wheel Kevin over the crossing. An elbow bend then takes me onto Railway Street where, while pedalling along the straight beside the park, I tell myself, as the Junction Primary School buildings draw closer, the passage through Hamilton and Hamilton South is near an end.

I have arrived early for the Yoga Aid Challenge. As I lock my bike to a pole outside the school, a vehicle or two pull into the curb, their female drivers arriving for the same Sunday morning reason as mine.

Lying on my back, my spine aligned to the spread of my legs and splay of my feet in what is commonly known as the corpse pose, and in a relaxed state, I experience an unexpected touch. Dave Morley, with practised fingers, gently prises open my hands and turns them facing upwards instead. It is a moment of intimate and careful realignment. One that invites a new intelligence to my limbs.

Hilary appears illuminated by the whiteness of her outfit. She explained her replacement status at the beginning of the programme soon after we entered the school demountable, "Deidre and Deb have gone to the farm." Hilary is representing Satyananda yoga today.

Along with her, at the front of the hall are a woman who teaches Ashtanga, Dave who tutors Iyengar, and a lady, who I'm told, practises at The Loft. Each takes a turn leading the class.

After the programme has ended, I thank Hilary. It's reciprocated. "Thanks for coming, Geoff." Then she and I hug.

Gerard and I have a friendship that is founded on arrangements. Lately, we have been meeting at The Kent on Sunday afternoons at 4:30 for constitutional drinks. On some of these days, we may encounter each other on the street outside. If I see Gerard's BMW turning in ahead of me, I will wait while he finds a park not far away. Should he arrive before me, I will usually find him at our preferred table on the stage, but our rendezvous rarely require much waiting for the other. And today, the minute hand on the clock beside the saloon entrance tells me what margin of time is left. Soon, on the half hour, Gerard walks through the door and we engage with a friendly handshake.

At the bar, the first of us to make the offer takes the shout.

"This is mine, Geoff. Two schooners of Cascade Light thanks."

Seated again, we sip a toast to our relative birthdays. Then each produces a gift. Gerard has brought his in a distinctive yellow and black plastic bag. As he passes the JB Hi-Fi purchase to me, I courteously place it on the table before me.

"And, I've got a present for you, Gerry."

Gerard also politely receives.

"Thanks, Geoff."

I remove the folded box-set titled *Waterways of Ireland* from the JB Hi-Fi bag. My friend informs me that he had to choose between this series and *Coast's* season centred on Ireland. I am quietly pleased that he went with the one he did, *Waterways of Ireland* looks like a fantastic exploration of the canals and rivers by boat.

"What a great choice. Thanks Gerry."

In return, Gerard unwraps the brown paper bag advertising The Book Grocer. As he does, he comments that he also goes into the Hunter Street shop to look at the ten dollar books. He observes that he has seen the Tim Flannery book. I register a note of conjecture in his voice, so diplomatically exploit the mutuality of the occasion by launching into a sales pitch.

"I thought that with you doing research into risk aversion about global warming you might find his book helpful."

"I don't always agree with what Tim Flannery says. But thanks anyway, Geoff."

And with this manner of congeniality, *The Weather Makers* becomes Gerard's territory, and *Waterways of Ireland,* mine.

Being my shout, our second beer is a middy of the same, Cascade Light.

It is Gerard's turn to cook at home tonight. This not uncommon pronouncement indicates that our afternoon at The Kent has reached the culmination of its allocated time. I accompany my more efficient friend to the exit as I am mostly prone to do. On the footpath outside we shake hands in farewell. Gerard departs in the direction of his BMW parked nearby, while I declare that I have, "... a little shopping to do," in the IGA.

56   What's New, Pussycat?

The term, heavenly piping and music playing, sits in my thoughts. In a few hours, after this morning's Greenie class at the Yoga Loft, Graeme and I will be giving our presentation. Graeme will be far from a yoga class, I am sure, possibly sleeping in after a night shift, or making the finishing touches to his share of the arrangement.

The exertion required to climb the stairs between the levels of office spaces and empty rooms to the top floor of the Sun building relegates my thoughts to an added extra. By the time, with heavy breath, I reach the reception, my humour has deserted me too. I am greeted by a friendly young woman at the desk.

"Happy birthday."

"I get it. You've got my birthday on your computer. Thanks."

"Enjoy your class."

"Thanks. I will."

All roads lead to the presentation. After lunch in the courtyard of the Hunter Building, I walk towards the library. Then along a hallway past drama labs and classes to the end staircase, where I turn left. Here, I meet a small group of early arrivals making small talk. Soon, Yin Gao arrives. She is short in stature and keen to lecture Chinese philosophy. We follow her up the corridor to the recessed blue door of lab HA110.

When Graeme enters the room, smugly prepared, it is only appropriate that he should sit beside me for the class. We have arranged that he will cover the overall philosophy of heavenly piping and where this fits with Daoist cosmology, and my talk will centre on the human experience of music in Daoism. His self-assurance is surprisingly validated.

He leads the presentation, confidently employing PowerPoint to present an overview. I have held reservations about Graeme's capability, his wavering on collaboration had generated doubt he would deliver. He concludes his emphatic spiel with a throw to me. A segue that is not as seamless as the theatricality suggests.

"Hello. My presentation on Heavenly Music and Music Playing will focus on the human experience. I hope to give examples that show how the power of music provides humanity with insight into the cosmos of Daoist philosophy."

Each topic of the discussion is partnered with an overhead slide on a screen, and all of these are formatted on a generic, pastel-green, wallpaper. On the lectern in front of me, the typed written report presents a list.

MUSIC IS ESSENTIAL TO HUMAN NATURE

"Our heavenly nature is to flourish.

Freedom is to hear yourself.

Heaven is found through forgetting yourself, things, and heaven.

Individual well-being is tied to common flourishing.

It is in human nature to experience the pleasures in music, beauty, sense of taste and power... it is not something that is learned.

The mind is agitated by inclinations and aversions and music and colours... yet it is moved by them to find the way.

The spirit loves harmony.

Being in harmony with all people is human happiness.

Being in harmony with heaven is the happiness of heaven."

As I read from my printed notes, and visit each of the seven slides, a satisfying correlation starts to evolve. There is a consolidation of validity, founded in my birthday I believe, that privileges today's presentation with an outcome of success.

I'd expected the 3:25 minute video of the two gentleman playing the zither and the flute to have a greater effect on the class. When I look towards Jason and Robert to garner their appreciation they both show blank expressions. I question how this celebration of humanity, so jubilantly expressed by the two Chinese musicians with their rollicking singalong and crowning fraternal laughter, can fail to induce in my classmates a response. While my online searches for exemplary eerie Chinese music discovered only compositions from later dynasties, I consider this video of a joyful recital aptly illustrates the human essence of Human Piping.

In my next example, the embodiment of music playing manifests itself in literature. I cite *Zhuangzi*.

"Beimen Cheng of the North Gate asks the Yellow Emperor about the powerful emotions he experienced while the music played. 'When I heard the first part, I became frightened, the next made me weary, the last perplexed me. I became alarmed and speechless and lost my self-possession.'

The Yellow Emperor replies. 'It was bound to affect you! Because, although performed by men, the music was attuned according to heaven.'

In open country, near Dongting Lake, as Beimen Cheng succumbed to the music of Xienchi, what was happening was an epiphany, whereby the man from the North Gate saw, simultaneously, what exists in music and what exists throughout all the elements in nature."

Slide Four is next.

THE HUMAN EXPERIENCE OF MUSIC ATTUNED TO HEAVEN

I have taken the liberty to create my own sub-classifications, and I can sense Yin Gao, powerful at her desk, ready to swoop and claim with academic talons any false arguments that may follow.

"Beimen Cheng's reactions are fear, fatigue and confusion. They are, respectively, products of music to inspire awe, to make solitary, and to make aware. These are states generated by sonic contradictions which direct, sequentially, radical observations of transition, magnitude, and meaning. This anxiety leads to a creative consciousness of heaven, and of the Daoist Way."

I notice Yin Gao sits composed, adding tallies to her rubric.

The cursor navigates to open Slide Five.

THE MUSIC OF EARTHLY PIPING

"Wherein, it is explained, that an energy of wind blows, always, through portals in nature, piping music to our human ears. Through these, only, can we conceive of the playing in heaven."

Slide Six.

THE MUSIC OF HEAVENLY PIPING

"Thus, one-ness is created. Sounds in heaven are produced by their own agency, they do not require an external wind, they are spontaneous and the player and the played are the same. Human, earthly, and heavenly piping, we find, are one with the Way."

Elemental single notes, diving then hovering like heavy drops of rain on dust or reins on a horse's neck, yearn and groan as each string suffers under the player's long, plucking, pressing fingers. We are hearing a Chinese folk song titled 'Wild Geese Descending on the Sandbank'. In the video screening, a musician is playing it on a plum-red zither.

"Following the opening notes, the player slides his fingers up and down the string without playing notes. A natural sound produced by the fabric of the string is sufficient. This ambient effect indicates the nothingness next to the something-ness in not only musical notation, but all things in creation. The harmonising life force of the music is said to be expressed in this shared quietness."

I conclude by quoting from *Lu's Spring and Autumn Chronicle* and the *Record of Rites*.

"Music... harmony... heaven... earth... yin... yang... earthly... ascends... heavenly... descends... heaven... earth... drum... thunders... wind and rain... four seasons... warm... with... sun and cool... with... moon... hundred transformations thrive... music... harmony... heaven and earth.

Thank you."

At the end of the seminar Graeme and I approach Yin Gao with mutual curiosity about our grade. She is unequivocal with her answer.

"A high distinction."

Keith opens his front door, and greets me heartily.

"G'day mate!"

"Hi Keith."

As he opens the door to let me in, we shake hands.

"Are you coming from uni?"

"Yeah. Had a big day today... had to give a presentation in Chinese Philosophy."

"Well, come on in to the computer room and take a seat."

I follow Keith into the first room on the left. Here, under the street-facing window, there is a table dedicated to a large computer and two waiting chairs. The central one is a high backed, black, office recliner, rather worse for wear, and the other is a squat, green, swivel chair in need of adjustment. Behind are shelves stocked with technical accessories such as camera tools and sundry works in progress. On either side of the room stand stacks of mainly pirated DVDs.

"Yeah... and it's my birthday today. And I just wanted to see a familiar face."

"Happy birthday, Geoff. It must have been rough giving a presentation on your birthday?"

"Oh, it was okay. I knew it was going to be on my birthday. It just goes with the territory. We went pretty well. Actually, it probably helped to make it to go better."

I sense a bemused look on Keith's face.

"Oh well, at least it's over."

"Yeah... sure."

I observe my old friend being drawn back to the screen beside him. An opened image of a bushland scene, saturated and therefore super-real, stares at us from his activated monitor.

Keith soon brings this latest adjusted photograph to the forefront of our attention. I wheel the swivel chair in closer to share his current preoccupation. I am conscious of the compromise in attending to a medium that stupefies me, however I accept the occasion as an opportunity for kindred sedation.

We talk for a while about this and other recent pictures Keith has captured in the field. While I make aesthetic appraisals in support of the artistry, Keith sources images that are indicative of the creative procedure. Apart from us considering what is apparent on the screen, there is not much further conversation.

I suddenly remember that with Dad being away, I had not found his cat this morning when I went to feed him.

"I had better get going, to track him down."

"Sure. You don't want to lose your dad's cat!"

Her housemate regards me for a moment from the hallway, and then defers to Lizzy who emerges from her room to answer the door.

"Hello I live across the road. (Knowing she knows where I live.) And I've been looking after my dad's cat whilst he's away. (Knowing she knows my Dad.) I've been looking for him for a while now, and it looks like he's missing. (I couldn't find him under Dad's bed, or under mine, or in the cupboard, nor outside, down the side of the house, or way under the house, he wasn't in the neighbours' yard, and Bradley, broad at his doorway, hadn't seen him around.) So, I was wondering if you had seen him about."

Although Lizzy does not appear to have seen the cat, I elect to furnish her with more information.

"He's not my cat. That's Pickles. (Knowing she knows Pickles.) You know the white one. He's an orange cat. Goes by the name of Buddy."

"Buddy. No, I haven't seen him around."

"Aww, okay. Thank you. Could you let me know if you see him around?"

"Sure. I'll let you know."

"Thanks. Well, I'd better keep looking."

"Good luck," she says in a direct, yet dreamy, tone.

"Thanks," I say with a doorbell sound.

A lost cat is a serious thing.

I grab the handrail and begin to mount the back steps where Pickles, in my path, sits stoically, meaningfully, as if against his better judgement, his gaze directed towards the locked garden shed. The shed!

The key turns.

The roller-door rises.

The afternoon light enters in.

A tense bundle of orange fur rockets out.

Pickles pulls a perturbed face at his liberated nemesis. He must have known that Buddy was stuck. I had foraged in there yesterday afternoon, He would have heard his laments as I had through the night, thinking it was a cat crying on the fence. He must have been busting with intelligence!

"Thank you so much Pickles, you have saved the day." I ruffle his furry half-ears in my hand then stroke his slick back hair. "You knew all along."

I sit with him on the back steps for a while, letting my thoughts soar, unbridled, into the sunset-lit clouds of the warm day. Relief and a gentler breathing happen, but I can feel his body stiffen. Pickles knows that somewhere out there Buddy is re-claiming territory.

"Ha-llo?"

"Hello Keith... it's Geoff ringing back. I just wanted to tell you... you know how Dad's cat was missing?"

"Ye-es... did you find him?"

"Yes, I did. It works out I'd locked him in the shed. I didn't know he was in there, and I'd been looking all around for him, even asking the neighbours, and then when I got back home, I noticed Pickles looking at the shed in a mysterious way and sure enough he was in there."

"It's lucky you found him, Geoff. It's been a hot day and he would have been dehydrated. He could have died if he was in there too long."

"Yeah, and I think he'd been in there since yesterday after-noon... that was the last time I can remember going in there."

"Well, it's good you got him out."

"Yeah, I reckon. And all thanks to Pickles for keeping an eye out for me. Oh, well, it was a happy ending. I'll talk to you later mate."

"Yeah. See ya later Geoff. Look after those cats!"

"I sure will."

"Hello again. I just thought I'd let you know that I found my dad's cat. I'd accidentally locked him in the shed."

Looks of comfort and then wry humour cross Lizzy's face.

"Good one."

Opening with the usual birthday wishes, Gemma speaks to me from her home down south. She and Dad have been house-hunting. A place in Yass has appealing assets, though she is inclined to settle for Cooma when the right place arises. According to her, it has been very helpful having Dad along as he knows what matters when it comes to houses.

I have been deliberating over whether or not to introduce today's incident into the conversation. The fact that Buddy's disappearance was solved makes giving another account of it seem unnecessary. However, perhaps because I lack other topics to impart, I elect to tell the saga one more time.

Gemma complies with my proposal to speak to Dad directly. He replies to each stage of my account by producing a series of listener's u-hums. When all that has happened has been recounted, and the consolation of the good outcome has been expressed, Dad has the last words about my part in his cat's story.

"You bet your life."

57   Hear My Song

Stephen's angel-like features appear sated when I tell him today is my birthday. After all, my tall friend already knows the ninth of September is a literary topic. His scholarly appetite for narrative in most things finds nourishment in those who are tellers of our own tales, so he is expectedly appeased. However, as someone who may be uncomfortable being seen as a character in a story as well as a workmate and friend, I am both honoured and ashamed to be in Stephen's company as one of my readers.

We leave the volunteers' lunchroom to make our way via the wetlands ponds to the tool shed. With my authorial dilemma put aside, I readily engage with Stephen, with whom I am surprised and pleased to be working again, in an informal, genial, and 'once a supervisor's' manner.

We are clearing some dead acacias from along a hillside in the bush-tucker garden. This involves accessing the imposing limbs on a steep slope, sawing them off at their trunks, dragging their lengths to clearings on the bank, and from these piles, carrying them to a track-side hollow where they are dumped.

During our lunch break in the volunteers' "dungeon", Trevor, in his self-confessed "two pound Pom" accent and with an open *Daily Telegraph* at his side, regales us about the forces that caused him to lose his job.

"One greenie kicks up a stink and they close the fucking place down."

The defiant pique with which I respond to his outrage is rationally advised that global economic factors are more likely to cause the closure of smelters such as Kurri, and the like, than are the actions of a single environmental activist. But the level of discomfort generated by Trevor's controlled anger does not recommend I attempt a spoken reply.

Stephen looks as though he has eaten something unpalatable he wants to remove from his mouth.

At the end of our day, my tall friend offers to drive me to the station.

On the way, he asks me whether my birthday is a special day for me.

The question is a loaded one, of course, as Stephen knows my birthdays are the subject of this series of short stories. As he steers the car into the drop-off area, I supply an answer that curbs any zeal for the occasion. After all, it was Jacko, who drives the tractor, who received the birthday goodwill today. My special day was characterised more by the ordinariness of labouring on a site that is largely overlooked, and being mindful of Stephen's disquiet since lunch.

"No, I'm really indifferent."

A working day is a bookended day. This morning, when Gemma had come in from the front half of the house, where Dad lives, to ask me what I was doing for the day, I had told her I would be leaving for the wetlands, and then had breakfast on my own. And now, this afternoon, as I pass Dad's kitchen window and screen door, I am coming back to Dad and Gemma's welcomes home.

After showering, I go next door, to the television event that dominates Dad's home life, and to experience his and Gemma's company. With an enthusiasm better than most Christmases I can remember, they present me with an object of special value, it is the complete series of *Little Britain*.

Faithful to our stroll and window shop last night, my sister and my father have returned to Hamilton Pawn Brokers today and bought the DVD box set. They swell with savvy as I show them my gratitude.

I announce, "I'm off to singing tonight," and ask Gemma, "Do you want to come too?"

She says, "I sure do."

They both explain they have had a big lunch today, "You go ahead and have some tea."

So the bookend is returned. As I sit at the dining table, in the back half of the house, I am having another meal on my own.

We are assembled in a loose circle. Gemma, standing diagonally opposite me, is a similar height to the woman next to her. Mary, with her wide eyes looking on from a broad and friendly face, has taken Gemma under her wing as she endeavours to sing the alto part. How orientating it is to observe the seemingly timeless appearance of my dear sister in the choir.

When I am leaning toward Dan, on my right, in order to vocalise the best way I can, and Colin's open eyes, after Dan's nearness, connect with mine, I discover I'm in a harmony with the basses more relevant than the one I usually share.

Perhaps there is something in the nature of family which provides an explanation for this current sense of purpose.

We have an unspoken understanding. Although our choir rarely features solos, a single member of the choir is always celebrated, accordingly, when they have a birthday. This is a ritual I know, as I have sung the song many times for others.

"Are there any more announcements?" Jacki asks.

"It's my birthday today," I say.

Gemma increases, proportionally, in a measure of support. Rebecca and some other tenors gleam, for a moment, before embarking on a common cause. Then all of the parts, in unison, join them in singing that most familiar chorus.

58   Islands in the Stream

Every day since I have been staying at Rick's at Sandy Beach, I have taken a morning walk along the sandy beach to the headland that lies ahead. At today's later hour, there are fewer walkers with less conviction, while an earlier rising brings to the constitutional course a larger population with more vigour in its stride. Accompanying dogs, in a range of breeds, activate their legs in time with their owners' rhythmic padding on the packed sand. One such owner, an older woman, has gone from greeting me, with her four-legged mate in tow, one morning to stopping and introducing herself while her terrier stayed until called, and then made a spirited dash back to her waiting hands. This morning I've started late, so I've missed her and the early crowd.

The sun is higher and is producing an irritating glare off the undulating, breaking waves. My walk has since approached the sand-banked mouth of the tidal inlet behind the dunes, with the allure of the flat rocks not far out to sea, and now returns with the shining water and rising sun hectoring me from the ocean side. As the day increases so does the sense of urgency to return not too late for breakfast with Rick, Rhonda, and my niece, Kerry.

Kerry and I share birthdays in the same week, hers is on the sixth, and this year it was on Sunday, the same day as Fathers' Day. My welcoming happy birthday downstairs was met with a slept-in counter response of her being over birthdays and guessing I would be too. A cynical enough reply, I thought, to concede at the time.

Dressed in an irreverent dressing-gown, torn in places, with her taut frame purposefully upright, Kerry looks as though she is reading from the same script as on Sunday. Her indifference to the topic has become my touchstone for relating to her today.

However, with Aunty Mary and Janet's tidings since noticed on my phone, I am inclined to think otherwise about birthdays.

From Aunty Mary. *Birthday greetings and have a happy day. We are off for a walk with the group about nine along the break-wall. Bought a new Holden Trax last week. Luv AM & UR xx*

From me. *Thanks AM and UR, hope you enjoy your walk. It's a beautiful day. Love, Geoff.*

I explain to Rick that the most recent message is from Janet, the lady for whom I do gardening in New Lambton Heights. "She is great. She always gets in touch with me on my birthday... they even give me a present at Christmas time. I'll just get back to her."

Hello Janet, am sitting in the sun on the verandah with my brother after a beach walk. Hello to the Koller family.

"I told her that I am sitting in the sun on the verandah with my brother after a beach walk."

I have joined Rick at the table outdoors. A trellised foliage forms a backdrop while, beyond, the depth of the backyard takes up the view. Rhonda emerges from the sliding door holding a cup in her hand. We make small talk while they have coffees and cigarettes. Buddy, exiled from my place to Rick and Kerry's care since his catfight with Pickles saw me hospitalised, endears himself to us until he is shooed from the table. I reflect on how much I would have enjoyed him being returned to Oliver Street, especially as he embodies a link with dad who is no longer alive. We discuss having lunch with Aunt Elizabeth, who has offered to drive up from Coffs Harbour to meet us.

"There's only one café in Sandy Beach... so it has to be The Lucky Chip." Rick states, with some irony.

Rhonda and Kerry, who has withdrawn to her domain upstairs, will follow us later.

My second walk today leads me onto the larger headland at the southern end of the beach. By accessing a track that rises from a sunbakers' nook, I can negotiate a route bearing across the slope below thick grasslands, and overlooking fishers' grottos flagged by Pandanus Palms. I am seeking solace in the empty coastal vista, but my return to nature is interrupted by a text message belling. Although this signals a necessary connection with my fellows, the phone's abrupt inclusion also heralds a withdrawal from experiencing oneness with the diverse, and unscrupulous, elements of the terrain I am entering. I momentarily park my backside on a tufted seat in order to respond to the message I have reluctantly paused to open.

From Gerard. *Happy Birthday Geoff! Hope you have a great day with the family. Almost warm enough for a swim! Cheers Gerard.*

From me. *Thanks Gerard, am sitting on a headland overlooking Sandy Beach, but a cool wind blowing. Thanks again, Geoff.*

The Lucky Chip reeks of boutique products, while offering a sufficient choice of gourmet-style burgers.

Outside the shop, a spacious timber deck looks over an extended park running parallel to the length of the beach. A couple of attractive, seemingly local, women are sitting at the table that benefits from the sun and appear ensconced in this desirable station. The only other table available, at the southerly side of the deck, is cloaked by the shadow of an umbrella, an appealing cover were solar protection sought, but serving today as a collaborator with the noon-time windy coolness and dampening air.

While Rick and I are waiting, he receives a call from Rhonda who informs him Kerry needs to go shopping, and she also won't be joining us for lunch because she needs to go with Kerry. When Aunt Elizabeth arrives, after parking across the road in her SUV, we relay to her the news there will only be the three of us.

I remove the navy blue lid, printed with a whale's tail and IFAW, and lift the polished silver emblem from the coffin-like box. The distinct shape of a whale's tail tied by a silver ring to a short rope loop identifies it as both a durable key-ring and a palpable keepsake. I relate to Aunt Elizabeth and Rick the meaning of AE's gift to the affecting observation I made yesterday of a whale and her calf breaching languidly off the coast as they kept pace with my south-heading walk. From a headland closer to their swim, I could hear the sound of the mam's guiding tail slapping on the water.

While Aunt Elizabeth converses, the train of her well-meaning dialogue is brought to a sudden halt, curbed by the clarion call of a new message signalled on her phone.

"This will be Gemma."

For a moment her snow-white hair and actress sunglasses are poised in downcast attention.

That she is correct entices me to play a prank.

From me. *Sitting with Rick and AE. See you prioritise your fave aunt over wishing your brother happy birthday. You're forgiven, G.*

And again from me. *It keeps you honest.*

From Gemma. *It does that. I've just had a load of wood delivered, much of which might actually burn by the end of next winter. I may be going snow-shoeing this weekend. Seems ludicrous after swimming in nearly 40 degree heat last week. Enjoy yourself today. Love to you all.*

Aunt Elizabeth has sent Gemma a teasing reply.

Gemma. *Thanks for dropping me in it bro! Duty before pleasure?*

Me. *It keeps you honest.*

Gemma. *Happy Birthday brother dear. Hope you are having a good day. Let me know when suits for a catch up phone call. Much love.*

Me. *Will be home on weekend, can talk then.*

During lunch, I am able to reach a position that meets with rays from the sun. By backing my chair from under the umbrella, I can now benefit from their warmth and gain consolation against the buffeting breeze. Although my satellite location does attract Aunt Elizabeth's counsel on sunburn.

Our aunt is certainly generous with her rationed time. She has recounted to us her rather strict agenda leading up to her arrival and following her departure. Rick and I are therefore aware that Aunt Elizabeth must make it back in time for her afternoon U3A course, that tomorrow morning she'll be undertaking, with her U3A walking group, a "good walk" along Moonee Beach, culminating in lunch at the tavern, and then she'll be motoring back to Coffs in the afternoon for a physio session. Her attention to itinerary brings to us a kindred sense of loyalty and security.

The walk across the road to AE's parked SUV presents a grateful return to movement and circulation. As we prepare to make our goodbyes, she announces she is not leaving quite yet. "I want to take a photograph of the two of you."

Rick and I wait while our pragmatic aunt opens her car to get the camera out. Re-joining us, she suggests we venture onto the beach, not the carpark, to pose for the shot. Agreeing to this, we undertake the short walk through the picnic area and along a track between two low fences. Deep beach sand obstructs the gain of our steps as we endeavour to reach a location beyond the shade of wind-breaking casuarinas. Halfway across, Rick and I assemble to satisfy Aunt Elizabeth's discerning camera eye. My brother hugs me with a heavy, cigarette-smoke laden arm while I reach around his burly neck, then together, combined in muscular obedience, we address AE's directed lens. As the shutter closes, I am conscious of the press of our whiskered cheeks, and how goofily wired I feel.

The image pleases AE. "I'll e-mail it to you Geoffrey, for when you get home."

The shopping excursion that Rhonda and Kerry were supposed to take has not yet happened. As no other plans appear to be evolving among the occupants of the two-storey house, I reckon on absenting from Rick, Rhonda and Kerry to spend the remaining hours of the afternoon on another walk before we leave for the Moonee Tavern.

This latest adventure carries a mode of unconscious escape. Replacing a roam on the headland again, I take the jungle path that crosses the land-mass at its neck instead. The sheltered track leads me to an eroded ravine and onto the lengthy beach that extends to the next high promontory. Not far along the cove, I notice a fellow following the shoreline in my direction. The man seems familiar, and as the distance between us decreases I become sure of his identity.

Yesterday, when I was taking leave from expeditionary strolling, and was sympathetically resting on a timber seat looking outwards, next to the vehicle access to the beach, and letting the figures and the scenery before me simply manifest, an older gent had joined me in checking the waves.

His conversation related as if he shared my present outlook. Standing nearby, he commented on the state of the surf. His manner implied I was taking time off work, and I guessed this was due to the hi-vis Bunnings Trade shirt I wore. He told me he was retired but continued to surf. That he would probably have another surf today. For the length of our chat, I felt the part of a middle-aged workman who was reading the waves, connecting with the unbridled sets on an earned break from the world that holds him down. Inhabiting the persona of this average bloke, for a while, lifted me out of myself.

The walker's suave good looks and stature, in conjunction with his preoccupied air, sees me revert to an inferior sensibility. Although I recognise him as the retired gentleman from a day before, I cannot revisit the commonality of our earlier topics of retirement and surfing. I lack the confidence to approach him, and the compromised look I surrender towards him is met with neither acknowledgement nor comment.

The lay of the beach seems run-of-the-mill today. The placement of driftwood and the repose of the dunes unravel in the direction I am taking with a sort of downplayed repetition.

Before leaving, I organised with Rick that I would carry my phone so they could notify me when they were ready for the tavern. Mindful of this arrangement, I employ my duty for being contactable by initiating the call.

"Hello Rick, it's Geoff... just to let you know that I've just reached the end of the next beach, and I'm heading back now... so, should only be half an hour."

"That's alright, Geoff. Kerry is still getting ready. Take your time... there's no hurry."

"Righto, mate. See you when I get back."

"Sweet."

The drudgery of trudging along the empty cove is accompanied by apprehension at the operatic irresolution being enacted between the upstairs and downstairs of my brother's castle. It is true, Rick's squatter's abode, compared to the territory Kerry claims above him, does not match the image of a ruler, but, like any man, my brother keeps a small kingdom of his own. I ponder the landscape before me, and grow unsure how this ocean, sand, and coastal vegetation can be assimilated into the household I am approaching.

What is on the television is as meaningless to me as leftover loaves in a bread shop I am only passing. I try, for a while, to position myself on the uncomfortable couch, but I am unsuccessful. Rick sits alongside me, yet he is somewhere unobtainable, my brother is used to Austar and the channels that it offers. I have drunk a can of Carlton Dry from the fridge, but to negligible satisfaction. The television, in front of us, inhales and breathes an emptiness over my soul, as if it wants to suck me into its circuitous tedium. We are enduring these conditions of an arbitrary wait, I believe, because of Kerry's obdurate preparations.

Driven by these testing thoughts, I have attached myself to a crosswords book placed open on Rick's bedroom cum office desk. Here lies my strategy to defeat the interminable wasting of our time. Alas, the clues are as difficult to follow as tailless dogs.

I make a few more kamikaze attempts, directing meanings into letters and locating targets on the grid. But, with my pen on lock, and in a turbulence that lifts me off the page, I launch from Rick's writing desk.

My legs in propulsion, on a compulsive walk around the

block, I make a declaration of war, against waiting.

Kerry has appeared at the bottom of the steps. My niece has at last reached a state that is ready for the Moonee Tavern. With her make-up applied, clothing decided, and hair done, she stands in the doorway and hurries us up.

I notice that Kerry has no shoes.

"I don't think they'll let you in without shoes."

"Do you *really* think I'd go out not wearing shoes?"

Her sharp reply digs under my skin. I climb into the back seat of the car, demeaned by the effort. The motor started, we back from the driveway and into the street. As the engine turns, the radio broadcasts Triple Jay. The youth station plays a frenetic rapping noise.

"Could you please turn that off? It sounds like a washing machine."

The surly register of my voice surprises me, I know it signals a worrying mood of pedantry. Having charged the atmosphere with my protest, we travel in the hushed interior of the car, produced by Rick's quick and learned attention to appeasement. Without music, we join the highway going south. Through my window, roadside landmarks and signage rush forebodingly by, into a night already near to closing time for the Moonee Tavern's bistro.

In a shockwave of emotion greater than the dramatic silence, Kerry bursts out a sudden announcement, she has forgotten to lock the doors to the balcony and the dogs could fall off. And there is no alternative other than to turn back immediately.

I fail to empathise with her imperative to enact a multiple rescue.

"Are you kidding? We are late enough as it is."

Kerry has become inconsolable. *She insists to Rick that he must drive her back to save the dogs.*

My resistance is unconscionable. *She tells me I am no longer welcome at their home and I can forget Christmas too.*

The following tirade against me being accepted at her home is loaded with expletives and self-righteous colloquialisms. I crouch like a boxer, sufficiently hunched in the backseat to take her incessant blows, the padded barrier of the seat serving as a glove.

Under attack, I fire off a volley of my own. "I can't understand a word you are saying, you talk like an American."

A heavy vibe ensues. Rick drives soundlessly, anchored to the wheel, Kerry sits beside him, she is speechless and focused on the dogs, and Rhonda and I in the back seat are wordless, constrained by our belts. As we enter the Moonee Tavern carpark we may be about to start a gunfight and sink in a hail of lead.

I utter to Rick, as father and daughter quietly reseat, "You're going back?"

His mumbled assent reveals the extent of his duty as her dad.

Rhonda and I are left to enter the waiting reality of the tavern's dining area on our own. We go through the motions of obtaining a couple of menus, in order to secure our meals and to have them ready in time for Rick and Kerry's pending re-arrival. The two of us take our places, as though we are players in the cumulative act of some unfolding tragedy. The sound of my scraping chair, Rhonda's hunched posture, the rigidity of mine, and our whispered concerns, must be speaking volumes to those seated elsewhere in the room.

I say of Kerry, to Rhonda, that she can be impossible to please.

"Well, I warned you."

A couple of things then happen together. The cooked meals are made available to our table, and Rick and Kerry approach the glass doors of the foyer. In a hurry, I tell Rhonda that I can't eat with Kerry, and, carrying my hot meal with me, I relocate to a different bar on the other side of the tavern.

The programme on television, with its merge of words and images, adds a meaningful narrative to my quandary. From an elevated screen, the artificial life has a commanding view over the purposeless scene where, in my remove from the others, I have staked a dubious autonomy.

Observing a couple of mates playing pool I think of an alternative take on events wherein I offer and Rick accepts to enter into a game. Turning my attention away, I further my investment in this hapless up-river excursion with a decisive stroke. The empty-hearted discussion at the bar that ensues sets the notion of sharing a celebratory beer on this birthday occasion aside, along with the passage of cues and balls over felt, for a schooner of lemon squash only. The barman humourlessly consents to the anomaly.

I can take posing like a shag for not a moment longer. Dismounting the barstool on my side of the partition, I leave the building by a secondary door. I understand that by going this way I run the risk of stepping onto an endless divorcing road. As I walk outside and face the night air, and begin to circumnavigate the carpark, I become increasingly aware of the pitfall of biting off more than I can chew. To reinforce this foreboding sense, I catch sight of Rick moving through the deserted interior I have just left. Caring on my behalf.

Rick sits opposite. At the same elevated table I'd occupied earlier in the story that I am still telling.

"This-is-very-difficult-for-me... I have crossed a line."

He listens to my explanation with a defeated look, his downcast face is streaked with lines of sadness and duress. He speaks few words. An unhappy realisation dawns on me.

Our brotherly love has died.

Because I have gone overboard, my brother's values for friendship and love have been undermined. Rick must therefore align with kindred spirits that assist his own well-being. The self-involved lemon squash man who reflects on his daughter's failings before him has become a person to whom it is difficult to relate.

I take a seat in the front next to Rick at the wheel. Kerry and Rhonda are seated behind, having already located themselves before we entered the car. We travel in silence, but despite this absence of discussion, Kerry's quietness communicates much to me. I believe my niece is contrite, mindful of the gravity of what has been gambled tonight, and I can only feel forgiveness in this moment of understanding her and of her understanding me. I regret that the occasion of my birthday has died a forlorn death. Sensitive to this sentiment, and as the vista streams ordinarily by, my thoughts turn to court the wretched maiden of defeat. But alas, this poesy of lily-white promise is soon pocketed and crushed under a recriminatory fist. Consequently, upon our arrival at the castle's driveway, it is decreed that they shall go their way and I will go mine.

"I'm going for a walk."

Alone, and on the dark beach, an alien landscape unfolds before me. Unseen waves, from an invisible ocean, shorebreak then disperse on the damp sand. Undulations, on the well-trodden beach, appear then disappear in strange caverns. I struggle onwards, barely able to contend with these obscure depths and hidden obstacles, any confidence in my steps confounded. What exists does so in fits of perception. All things, without me, collude to ignore my feelings, and the night beach does not want to be a friend. An outrage, inside me, erupts and rides over their uncooperative pact, and swears loudly in drowning it.

"You rotten bastard!"

My words are aimed at my neighbour. Not miles to the south in Dad's old half of the house, but stationed in the shrill oblivion that engulfs me. That I am staggering, fist-fighting and praying into with clubbing hooves. Even during metamorphosis, it strikes me as odd my wrath is hurled at him. His name torn randomly from a taunting, nebulous phonebook. I stumble, aggrieved, carrying his effigy clinging to my torso like a segmented crab.

I've landed in long grass. My animal eyes have steered me off the sealed road to this location outside of utility. This is a newfound land of invention. Here is a place where I can go to disobey rules and dwell as an abnormal being. Among the lifeless drapery of leaves, I can see the mowed expanse to the houses and street as a plateau separate from the overgrown trench on its fringe I occupy.

It is here where I will make my stay.

Yet, I am in doubt about how long this antipodes of normality will seclude me with its nocturnal veil. At another end of the long paralleling park, where it lifts into headland scrub, I can imagine kangaroos embedding themselves in a scene of ownership. I don't look like a kangaroo. Other thoughts are lost in a masticating stupor. While, high above my head, the field of stars hold no interest. This must be the end of my world.

Kerry has an issue with the door to the garage downstairs making a noise heard too much upstairs, so, like a sneaking individual, I avoid her ire by taking the side path and back steps to where Rick lives. I appear in his small living area, where he merges with a television programme.

"I had a little sleep."

My brother is immersed in a reality series set on fishing trawlers in the Bering Sea. He has told me how much the show means to him, that he had cried during an episode when one of the Alaskan fishermen died. I know that in an ideal reality, where our relationship sailed smoothly, we would be watching *Deadliest Catch* together.

"I'm off to bed."

"Goodnight, Geoff."

With an unconscious mind your emotional truth rises in you, if it holds a great feeling of remorse, you will break down and cry. Deep in the post-television silence of the night, this happens to me. My head, outweighed by defeat, surrenders control to a begging heart and a beggar's body. Their reunion, in a bout of moaning, can be seen as the laborious sensation of a return to language. I let the moans carry me for a time. I am troubled, though, by the sound of movements navigating on the floor above. Could Rhonda and Kerry be privy to my very private despair?

I wake again later in the night, this time in an instant of cumulative horror and regret. From a mattress bed on the floor, where my brother sleeps having given up his room, from an upturned nose in the dark, loud snoring plays a sorrowful lament. Near to Rick, one of Kerry's beagles also snores, in accompaniment on the lounge.

59 I Wanna Be Well

Looking through the mouth of the tunnel, I see the struggle of the night, wracked with tiredness and slumped on the tracks. Around my sick bed, the strain of emphatic coughing still lingers. I have been trying to decide whether to surrender my ticket to *Othello* to someone else, before it is too late. And that someone has become Patricia from Laughter Club who might, possibly, have an interest in going. But the deliberation has expired with the choice to keep the purchased ticket as an investment that is mine only. I have contemplated too far to think about it any other way.

Rising from the disused mine that has been my sleep, I reckon with the day as though most of it has already been experienced. The first Station of the Cross is Hamilton Station, followed by the train to Sandgate and the wetlands.

I have a history of entering the Hunter Wetlands unwell. The property greets my running nose like a massive handkerchief, it takes its snotty discharge as a strategy toward self-improvement. Encouraged thus, I go about my business.

The nesting freckled ducks are counted. Meanwhile, their male suitors compete, making claims with their *true* red bills on territory in and around their freshly-filled dishes. Sometimes, the birds cock, with their brown to black eyes, an uncertain look that causes me to speculate about our mutual interest. I notice rat droppings are polluting the bench top, so task myself to place baits there later.

Putting the baits behind the thick rubber edging that bends under the sink requires me kneeling on the sodden matting where we feed the ducks. As I fasten the perfumed wax blocks to the wire fence, I can feel an unhygienic dampness soaking through the thinning drill cotton of my work pants, both at the shins and the knees.

Seated, with my legs outstretched outside the lunchroom door, I text Gemma a reply. *Thanks Gemma, sunning myself at the wetlands, then early mark and Othello tonight, but cough! Thanks about White Album.*

Across the way, I notice John's father, Reg, tending to the blue shipping container where the Segways are stored. He has just opened the door. He emerges from the container, and as he crosses the road in the direction of their small downstairs office, he recognises me with a friendly greeting. I explain to Reg that I am drying off my trousers in the sun and ask him whether they have a tour on this afternoon. Instead, he answers, they are bringing the vehicles back to the shipping container. Soon after, John and Stephen arrive in the carpark with their extra-large trailer and begin riding the scooter-like transporters down through the open gates.

With the vehicles stored away, Stephen approaches where I am sitting. Our meeting today is uncannily timely. The occasion of my birthday spent volunteering at the wetlands two years ago, in 2014, was also graced by his presence.

For a while, we are locked in conversation about the Buzzcocks gig I attended earlier in the year, although, I am keen to introduce the topic of my reading *Lord Jim*. This is relevant to our friendship because I am reading Conrad's novel due to Stephen's heartfelt recommendation.

When I make my proposal that "Patusan… where Lord Jim had his fortress… is in Aceh," Stephen replies with an admission, "I did not know that," and furthers his observation by saying, "I still remember the lessons from that book."

Our discussion in the midday sun is warming. I am reminded of a scene from Sam Peckinpah's film, *Pat Garrett and Billy the Kid,* where Bob Dylan's "Alias" sits on a farm fence and imparts home truths to a captive listener. Having turned fifty-nine, I believe this kind of ego sunbake can be permitted.

I let Rohan, my supervisor, know I am knocking-off early. When I tell him it is my birthday and I am going out to the theatre tonight, he replies, "You are full of surprises."

Before leaving, I bid The Runt a short farewell where he is kept in the reptile sunning shelter outside the dungeon door. He was returned to his mother and siblings in the nursery shelter, but he was likely bullied there, as he has lost condition, his feathers are damp, and he looks forlorn. As a consequence, our most sympathetic freckled duck is again under cover, in the shade, waiting out another day in captivity.

As I am going, a call for someone to launch a two-seater canoe comes over the radio. As David offers to exit his office to perform the duty, I make my shy escape.

I confess to myself that sitting opposite her forward facing seat at the end of the carriage is voyeuristic and meant. She is too voluptuous to ignore, like a big, ribboned gift. Over the young woman's large expanse of bare crossed leg, forthright cleavage, and barely opened mouth, my eyes scan and rest and meet hers, looking away. Inside my pants, a universal pulse stakes a claim.

I depart the train, carrying her sexual bulk with me, inside my mind.

I bring her home, placing her lingering prize onto a towel spread on the carpet, into my body, with my head on a pillow on the floor. This is the passion that brings a woman to the cushioned earth.

In such sudden movement, a force exists, as does a quiet need for rest. My physical self is at odds with itself, its impulse for conquest is in dispute with my male body, rigidly erect, on its back on the pillow and the towel. When I pull into the station, as I always do, my conflicted driver feels a real pain and strain in his furrowed brow. With ejaculation, a person of solace is often sought. But who comes at that moment, as my remembered nurse, is to my surprise and disappointment, Stephen.

Heavy-headed after an evening meal, I am tending to unfinished business started this morning at 09:42:08.

Thanks Rick, at Wetlands, home after 3

Righto, call this Arvo, have a good one

I feel obliged to honour Rick's reply, and mean to contact him within the terms of time I have left before leaving home for *Othello*. The digital clock, inherited from dad's bedside table, gives me half an hour.

I phone Rick from my landline. He sounds disappointed, informing me it was his intention to wait until after dinner before he called me. I explain that I am phoning him now because of the play. I am advised that Kerry cannot participate in the call because she is upstairs with her dog, Gigi. The animal is recovering from the paralysis tick that was central to Kerry's emotional state when we talked three nights ago, on her birthday.

"I'll be down there in two or three weeks for a few days."

"That'll be good, we can catch up then."

"I was talking to Chris at trivia the other night and he told me that Sam Chupachuck is playing drums with him in Spoonbender," I add, in a schedule-induced, higher register.

"No I didn't know. He's kept that a secret from me."

"You should take full advantage of this insider information."

"I will," he chuckles, good-naturedly.

The stage is furnished with a minimalist set, consisting of a few chairs and a table. Atmospheric music passes through the auditorium, raising our expectations for the performance that will soon inhabit the vacant platform. But a discombobulated feeling, borne since the above-mentioned, misguided masturbation, combined with today's illness re-emerging for a second shift, causes me to savour the viewing corridor before me with a readiness built on threat. And I am dismayed when the sight-line to the theatrical frame is unceremoniously blocked by a seated head.

Act one, scene one of *Othello* commences with boardroom efficiency. Two characters plot a manipulative course central to the drama. Although I may lean my head to one side sufficiently to observe them, the loss of sound over the Civic Theatre's seating is such, that by row T, I cannot rightly interpret what the actors have to say. Bell Shakespeare's costume designer has opted for the autumn range. The cast, like models, exhibit a series of tableaus designed to strengthen the brand. The men are bulked, yet their voices are small. The leading lady, Othello's Desdemona, is the play's main selling-point. I crane my neck, to imagine a crooked stage level, and strain to hear speakers beyond reach, while lurgy pervades all. A storm at sea, a modern, loud, calamity, showcases backstage creatives schooled in sound and lighting, and along with onstage mouse-avoiding, chair-standing, temporarily wakes me from my mordant state, and discomfort too. Othello's duped and rising jealousy, aimed specifically, and harshly, at his God-fearing spouse, has reached under my skin and increased my curiosity for the play's second half. But, alas, the enduring obscuration of the theatre in front of me has already produced a resolve to stay no more.

"I'm not feeling well. I'm not staying for the rest of the play. You can have my seat, if you like. You might get a better view."

I speak to the partnered young woman beside me, for whom I have felt an uncomfortable empathy as she has struggled to experience the show as well. The young woman responds graciously.

"Thank you... I hope you are feeling better."

I make a reasonable exit down a short flight of interior stairs. I recognise the strangeness of leaving a theatre only at interval. However, the palpable, liberating air that meets me at the bus stop, is a reassurance I have made the right choice.

Ensconced on board the government bus, and motoring through to Hamilton, a declamatory letter, with phrases such as "dishonoured the nature of theatre", composes in my head. Getting off at Hamilton, the driver returns my parting words with his own gesture of support for the people's revolution.

60   American Pie

Gemma raises her head from the pillow and blankets proffered on the floor. Her bed is under the dominant, jet-black face of the turned-off television screen, between that edifice and the lounge.

"How did you sleep?" I ask her, with some concern.

"I had to wait until the movie finished."

I imagine a gossiping Hollywood blonde selfishly, loudly, demanding attention from the septuagenarian and octogenarian elders who occupied the lounge-room until the film's end.

"Happy birthday, brother."

Since we arrived at Aunt Elizabeth's yesterday afternoon, a measure of adaptation has delivered me to this receptive, supportive chair placed in the corner of the front room. I am afforded from here a good view of the interior of AE's customised Coffs Harbour home. I have procured out of the kitchen a bowl of cereal doused with milk, not refrigerated, mildly unpleasant, poured from the Tetra Pak appointed as the breakfast supply. This was followed by a slice of toast spread with Vegemite. Now I drink honeyed black tea from a great black mug labelled "Mathilde" and "children are maggots".

Uncle Ray emerges out of the sizeable bedroom where he and Aunty Mary have slept the night and passes the toilet and bathroom then turns to greet me with a fragile vociferousness befitting his age. As he approaches, I rise to receive his kind and gentle hug, a morning embrace on the occasion of my 60th, given with an expiration of stale breath that is accepted without prejudice.

"Who'd have thought?" he cheerily announces, meeting my eyes with his. "Your mother and father would have wondered if they'd see this day... They're here with you today."

Aunt Elizabeth, resplendent in an electric shock of truthful white hair borne over a pink dressing-gown, delivers into my hands a gift. Covered in brown paper printed with native animals, the wrapping evokes a memory of a childhood picture-book I had about piccaninnies.

"I guess you guessed this was a book."

I unwrap the gift, carefully preserving the brown paper, to reveal a paperback with the title *Girt*. The same book had been the topic of discussion when AE had told me over the phone she was waiting for a copy to be ordered through the library. At the same time she had been secretly securing a new copy for me. I open *Girt* and, in a gesture of inclusion, read aloud the sentences from the bottom of page 34.

"This is, of course, only one view of Aboriginal history. Before we consider alternative theories as to how Australia's unoriginal non-inhabitants didn't not come here and what they didn't not do after their failed non-arrival, we should talk a little about armbands."

Aunt Elizabeth's card, previously withdrawn from a hand-decorated envelope featuring my initials "G...C...N" outlined by a cloud, with an image of a sailing boat vested in a calm scene, has equated my being with being special.

The next to step into the significant space represented by my seated self today is Aunty Mary. Her tribute is less flattering. In keeping with the Flaherty girls' sense of frank irreverence and mirth, the gift-bag she produces, she candidly admits, is labelled mine over cousin Evan's from Christmas last year. Like Mum before her, the older of the two surviving Flaherty sisters has an intrinsic ability to dethrone self-importance.

Out of the pre-presented offering, I fish a tub of men's shower gel that is, apparently very good, a neat, grey, bamboo print surf-shirt that is, befittingly small, plus another book, titled *Aussie, Aussie, Aussie*, which maintains the history trend. In addition to *Girt, The Charge,* a new book on Beersheba, has been gifted from Gemma, and now forms a platform for the small pile beside me.

Undermining the material posed by these fresh editions are thoughts lingering on pages of *Lasseter's Diary*. Therein, the dying explorer gives an account of his threatened demise due to miscommunications, mis-shots, misadventures and mysteries, all under the jurisdiction of a territorial tribe. It can only end badly. I have been engrossed in reading Lasseter's re-imaged troubled handwriting throughout the cornered morning.

To Aunt Elizabeth's busy and turned back, I say, "Thomas Keneally has written a big, serious, history of Australia."

Evan surfaces from the same end of the house as did his father. He has, for the meantime, separated himself from the hypnotic screen that now furnishes him with information.

In a tone of journalistic matter-of-factness, he tells us that the biggest earthquake ever recorded, "8.5," has occurred off the coast of Mexico or, "… one of those smaller countries in Central America to the south of it." And on the San Andreas Fault Line. With a following tsunami in Hawaii, Tahiti, and New Zealand expected. Also Hurricane Irma is rotating in the Caribbean and is the size of Tasmania with 300kmh winds, and two more storms have joined her.

My cousin proceeds to turn on the blacked-out wide screen in the lounge-room. His measured reportage is supported by footage of an emphatic swirl of cloud around an unblinking eye, a satellite's view.

Evan continues with his steady appraisal. Already the Doomsday prophesiers are citing old writings that have predicted a similar culmination of catastrophic events.

Meanwhile, Mexican voices are giving their own commentary on the 24-hour news channel.

"Hello Rick... thanks mate... how's Inverell?... Gemma is picking Natasha up from the airport at twelve-thirty, so one-o'clock for lunch should be just about right... thanks, see you both then."

Happy birthday Geoff. Have a good day with the family. The Tiges had a great win last night. Gerard

Thanks Gerard, and congrats to Tiges!

The lyrics to 'You Are My Sunshine' occupy my mind with a singing voice. And, as I cross Park Plaza's impervious carpark, my thoughts return to the uplifting song's hidden lament. They sympathetically reflect on those persons close to me who have undergone a background demise. Such as Arlo, when he was about to pass. Or Mum, when she was losing her struggle. The catchy Americana tune has carried a sting in its tail ever since. I acknowledge these are off-kilter thoughts.

At the counter of Beer, Wine and Spirits, the proprietor openly protests about his business having to re-instate plastic bags due to the brunt of older customers complaining about their withdrawal from use. I submit to the owner's tirade, while loading the weight of a Coopers' six-pack into an obedient backpack.

Relieved to be back outside Park Plaza shopping centre, Gemma and I stroll laden, and semi-confidently, towards the location of our car. As we navigate the rows of parked vehicles, we notice a migrant Australian dad singing to his joyfully piggy-backed daughter, "Happy birthday to you. Happy birthday to you."

I am standing alone in the kitchen after unpacking our groceries. I am spending a moment looking at a photograph of Mum and her sisters taken in front of their ship before they sailed. Mum does not look well in their company. She brought me into the world sixty years ago, today.

I ask Uncle Ray, seated by the front window, about the book he has in his hands. He is more than happy to discuss the author's thesis on Noah's flood. When the whole world went under water, Mount Ararat, being too high to land on, was unlikely to be where Noah's ark was grounded. And, on top of this, the book is evidence for Solomon's temple's ruins. I show him that I am listening, albeit not quite following, by telling him about a television documentary I saw on the dimensions for the base of the Tower of Babylon. That, due to an extended drought in the region, inundated swamps had dried and afforded unprecedented access for a perennially scouting archaeologist. Uncle Ray returns to the story of the Templar Knights. He outlines the Jewish movement from Israel to Babylon, with their attaining of permission to return, and their hostilities with the Samaritans on the opposite bank of the river. I am imagining the scene when my mobile phone gives an interruptive ring.

I step outside the house, leaving Uncle Ray in the lurch and in a midstream of thought, to take Stephen's call. His timely recognition of my birthday is thankfully received. While Stephen tends to my interest in a downtime from taking Segway tours, I endeavour to provide him with a picture of the company I am keeping.

"Chatterboxes... crossworders... and readers."

As the words leave my mouth, I wonder and have doubt about whether I am painting Uncle Ray, still seated inside, with a wet paintbrush.

Stephen, tellingly, asks me if I have heard of a recently released recording where the musician has composed a different song for each year of his life. I answer that I have heard of it, and that I think it is carries the title of *The 50 Song Memoir*. Stephen tends to agree. I continue speaking on the topic of the recording through recollecting knowledge of a particular song that describes the artist as a young boy adrift in a canoe with his hippy parents. I provide another fact with the information that the musician said he found his stride when he discovered the music of New Romantics. Stephen sounds surprised. When I recommend Lambchop's idiosyncratic style, he announces, "I'm looking him up as we speak." We both agree that we should catch up.

No sooner does our conversation finish than I am observing Gemma and Natasha pulling into the driveway. They maintain an exact parking distance from the SUV already standing there. As mother and daughter unbuckle and disembark from the car, I am given time to navigate to the other side and give my niece a 'welcome back' hug.

"Happy birthday, Uncle Geoffrey."

While I was speaking with Stephen, Rick has experienced a missed call to my phone, so he has spoken to Gemma instead. When we talk, my brother expresses his displeasure at finding Kerry, with his arrival at Sandy Beach at eleven-thirty, still in her dressing-gown. This was even though he had told her from Inverell he was on his way, and to get ready.

"It may only be me at lunch. Kerry is getting her hair ready for tonight."

A text, sometime later, indicates a qualified success. In that, after half-twelve, he is making an egress from out of their house and into the car to join us. Albeit, *Start without me.*

With Rick in transit, I can concentrate on being celebrated by the family members who are present. I join them where they are gathered around a lunch table under Aunt Elizabeth's commented-on new awning.

Aunt Elizabeth pours us sparkling wine. Natasha, who, before going overseas, worked as a barmaid at the Marlborough Hotel in Newtown, reminds us that it is incorrectly identified as champagne. We receive the alcohol in small plastic goblets to drink a toast and sing Happy Birthday. Then, AE follows with a flattering speech that I am, through humility, opaque in believing. With my second cup, I sense a negative effect looming. Suddenly, I feel the placement of Rick's hand on my shoulder.

"You said start without you. But there is plenty left." I blurt.

After lunch is eaten and the plates and leftovers have been removed from the scene, "the cake that men like" is offered to the table. There are two candles pricked into the mortar-like casing of caramel fudge icing. The larger wax candle is blue with a red number sixty and the smaller is yellow and has a white wax star. They are both accompanied by a small brass-handled bell. Having puffed out the dual flames effectively, I am alerted too late by AE's injured comment that the odd little bell is the snuffer.

"You are meant to use it on the candles!"

Evan emerges from where he is following the latest on the

Mexican disaster to join our spirited reprise of the birthday chorus. Even I sing to myself this second time.

I then cut the cake. But I am unused to wielding a slicing knife. Nor am I competent in measuring the sizes of the slices. In cutting from the middle of the cake to shape a block I call an oblong, a debate begins about whether an oblong is a rectangle.

"It is a big slice," I attempt.

Somewhat driven, Evan adds that my primary slicing has engendered secondary divisions with geometric confusion. Despite this criticism, I have two of them. And two caramel tarts.

"I am sorry, Geoffrey. Your cake has turned out a brick," Gemma later tenders.

"Another brick in the wall," I smartly offer, in recognition of the Pink Floyd anthem we endured together on our drive from Newcastle yesterday underneath stands of tall trees along the Pacific Highway.

We elect to take our photographs under the canopy of Aunt Elizabeth's new awning.

Aunty Mary and I pose before a printed banner, images of *HAPPY BIRTHDAY* and clustered balloons sticky-taped to the brick wall.

In mock sibling rivalry, Gemma and I torment the skeletal integrity of a clammy chicken wishbone.

We notice that in the second, and decidedly better, picture taken in front of the party banner that I do not show much of my ears. And that Aunty Mary does not have much ears either. Aunt Elizabeth then reveals, by tucking back her soft white curls, that she has one ear pronouncedly bigger than the other.

"Great Aunt O'Leary used to get drunk under All Campbell's Bridge, and yell obscenities at people walking overhead."

Her family genealogy, AE informs us, goes back to Jewish and Prussian forebears as well as the Derry Irish.

Aunty Mary then explains why the O'Learys in Bingara had four Catholic children before the fifth became an Anglican. It was because their parents fell out with the town's Catholic priest that our Anglican side of the family came into being.

A staunch sense of Irish tradition remained alive in my grandfather, Pop Flaherty. His treasured fiddle is stored, to my thrill, in a corner of Aunt Elizabeth's dining room. She shows me the delightful instrument perched upward beside a stack of records. Without strings. Without a chin rest.

"He used to play a jig on it."

"When I was in Donegal I went to a folk village on the coast, and they had demonstration cottages from the history of Donegal. And in one of them I took a double take, because Pop's likeness was sitting on a chair playing a fiddle. It was a wax statue of Johnny Doherty who was credited with bringing Irish fiddle music down from the mountains."

Aunt Elizabeth had earlier made an offer to those of us who may become her inheritors. "Make a list of five things you would most like to have... while I still have them."

I ask her if I could include the fiddle.

Rick is about to leave, to return to Kerry at Sandy Beach and help his daughter with feeding animals. They will join us later tonight for the Tex, Don, and Charlie concert in Bellingen. I ponder whether to give my brother the remaining bag of roasted sugared almonds before he goes. I think twice because the bags were specially offered to me as a birthday gift from Hamilton Thai Massage.

Rick says he knows the place. "The one above the barber's."

I repeat an explanation delivered at an earlier juncture of the day, that the home-made treats in the bags are tokens of their Buddhist beliefs. But I cannot speak the trains of thought that follow our sayings of goodbye.

Yvonne chased after me onto the crossing on Beaumont Street with her hands full of more sandwich bags packed with sugar almonds, calling, "Geoff!" When she caught up with me, all cheer and fluster, she said, "Nadia said to give these for your birthday." The male voices from the verandah of The Kent drunkenly adding their unrequired support, "Hey, have you got some for me too?" Her thanking smile added to the sincerity of my neighbour who, when I bade him farewell yesterday morning, said to me from his open doorway, "James said happy birthday." James had said *Sex and drugs and English Literature, hey Nic?*, back on my 21st birthday in 1978, when I returned from studies in Armidale to the apartment he shared with Don and the others, *Eldnur* at the top of Wolfe Street. My thoughts cascade to last weekend when, at my request, Patricia and Brian, in a fresher memory, converged on me with elated energy in transmission of a Laughter Club *whoosh* for my up-coming sixtieth birthday.

All these harboured signs and signals leading up to today. Their sense of significance. I think some things are best kept to myself.

Unlike the activity of scrolling and scoring a life story, the weekly undertaking of Mungo MacCallum's cryptic crossword warrants conference. With last weekend's *Saturday Paper* open on the second last page, and Gemma adding her decryptions alongside mine with words spoken out loud and words written down, the puzzle's mute gridlock is broken. However, some solutions are remembered. I confess that those entered in a twin copy of the paper, folded in a backpack in the spare bedroom I have borrowed, help feed our success, make me look quicker in thought than I am.

From three metres aft, Evan floats correct interpretations of untied conundrums, drifting them onto us and into our detective moorings. His cryptic lucidity, plus an exemplary vocabulary, have already piloted his mother, Aunty Mary, into her puzzling port, and now they resource him with the necessary craft to take on the summit of Mt *Times* Cryptic in *The Weekend Australian*.

"I have only solved it twice in the, what, eight years I've been doing it."

I am trying too hard. Face down in my own narration, in an effort to educate my inadequacy when I become too complicated, I am reading *Feeling Good* again. The practical instructions for defeating depression are not suitable reading on a party day, I know. Yet I concentrate.

The author presents a case study where his fellow American recounts her dilemma of facing presumed insurmountable odds. Paralysed by internalised barriers, she is unable to move from her room. David D. Burns dons his therapist cloak and shows her to the door, leading her by the hand to a columned chart configured on the floor. Here we can read her interests, documented and sub-headed, under helpful checklists. Mary sees the light. We are on your journey too, Mary. Although you were sad, and lived in America in the 1970s, and David's rules, though rote, were no doubt real for you, your struggle is ours, too.

"How's your 'William McInnes' going, Gem?"

"It's good. He writes about families really well. He tells this story about how he misses his son's graduation show and then lies about going to his wife. His son tells her he wasn't really there, so they play along with him pretending he'd gone. There's a lot of humour in it but a lot of heart as well."

"What are you reading, Evan?"

"Oh, it's just Manning Clark's history of Australia. I'm just picking through it. I got it off Aunt Elizabeth's bookshelf."

"I saw him in Melbourne once... or he saw me. I was talking to a Russian fellow next to a fountain and I noticed this man staring intently at us. And it was Manning Clark. He must have seen something in us that represented Australian society at the time."

Uncle Ray is either asleep or awake in his chair. The pages of Noah's flood are open on his lap.

Natasha curls in a somnolent state. Her back faces the doorway as she turns onto the comfortable second bedroom bed.

The afternoon undergoes that warp where boredom, becoming the hand that moves the chess pieces of our lives, quietly transfers us from one time to another.

I step into the lounge-room. I paddle into the wake made by Gemma's raised voice. The game is mostly played. Her offensive has nearly taken the territory of our square-mouthed aunts and uncle.

"It is an act of bastardry to even call same-sex marriage an issue at all!"

The others hold that people are used to a certain way of thinking and they are not about to change their beliefs.

Gemma is a jug approaching boiling. Rapid bubbling and sighs of steam emit from her aura. The others are at one with the furniture.

Evan makes both an entrance and an exit.

"I'm gay."

I follow him off stage.

"Bob Katter would have something to say about you using the word that way."

Rick calls. Grudgingly thankful, he announces that Chris Evans has finally come through with extra tickets for tonight's show. They'll use them. He asks me what time we are thinking of leaving. They'll drop by on their way.

"Sorry, we can't afford to wait... meeting us here... if Kerry's running late... to claim the seats at the theatre... we have to leave at six thirty. We'll see you there."

The broadcast of the Mexican story is continuing in the now empty lounge-room, the board having been cleared after the same-sex discussion. The super-text captions are out of sync with the better said, but overly-loud, commentary. I find them confronting, and the broadcast media overwhelming, so escape to the smaller television in the dining area.

The early news, on the better-managed ABC, is followed by *The Drum*. A full-figured, bald-headed man in an open-necked shirt says something, well, about something. Evan is with me, facing the screen on a three-seater lounge. His closeness adds to the discomfort caused by the deepness of the lounge and the poor posture it produces. I must uproot and leave, only to return soon after and occupy, erect and lady-like, the floral patterned armchair set back from where Evan is viewing.

Prior to sitting, I had considered explaining to my stolid cousin that I had needed to relocate due to the lounge being too uncomfortable. A weighted sensitivity I thought, and difficult to express.

"Is it okay to turn the tee-vee up a bit?"

We have two spare tickets to the show.

Evan elects not to attend. "I'm feeling ordinary."

There is an air of ceremony in my dressing for Tex, Don, and Charlie at the Bellingen Town Hall. A blue-checked flannelette goes on top of the black printed Ned Kelly tee, comfortable blue jeans pull up over cotton underpants, brown socks feed into Dad's black Colorado shoes, and topping the penultimate fawn and navy-blue armed jacket goes the green-and-grey striped beanie.

"Do you think it will be cold in the hall?"

"Nah, it will be warm." Gem knows.

In the car on our way to Bellingen, Gemma expresses bemusement at the level of venom in her argument with Uncle Ray and the Aunts. At how unjust their conservative attitudes are.

"It should not be an issue."

With her hands on the wheel, my sister reiterates her opposition to the postal survey on marriage equality. We share a misgiving that recalcitrant values may hold ground. From the front seat, Natasha offers that the majority of her friends have voted YES to the survey. Gemma and I respond to this with some relief. If the younger adults have their say it should be enough to get the message through.

We cross over the broad, night subdued sweep of the Bellinger River, under the historic overpass where Arlo once left a cache of dope in a pair of old boots for his mate Andy to later discover, and wend our way west, over hill and dale, to Bellingen town where Gemma and Arlo, years ago, brought their children to grow.

Turning onto a backstreet takes us in the vicinity of the great trees where the Bellingen markets are held. The darker area below their grand trunks holds memories for Natasha, and she reminisces, "My first singing gig... under those trees."

"And your hand-made jewellery," I recollect.

I have two surplus tickets. "These things happen," I explain to the two crisp and worldly ladies seated at the reception table of the Community Hall. My statement of defeat is surprised by one of the ladies suggesting, "Why don't you try putting them in the window to sell?"

She goes further, offering her pen to enable me to write a message on the back of the printed receipt.

Two Tickets for Sale – 0422589186.

Thanking her, Gemma, Natasha and I, attend to securing the note by wedging it between the trim and window of the front door so it faces onto the street.

We take our seats in a front ranking row and occupy two more than our three to allow for Rick and Kerry's pending arrival. As I look around, it becomes evident to me that the audience meeting tonight is notably select. An adult society has evolved in Bellingen that represents the success of my generation's counter culture. Arriving to their seats they sparkle with lucidity. Either grey-haired or with autumn hues, in weather-suitable clothes, carrying the hallmarks of a healthy longevity, in manners of discussion, in transmissions of intelligence, they create throughout the space of the hall a lively, knowledgeable sense of community.

My phone rings. I answer promptly, because that is what one does, to see unfamiliar numerals and hear a gentlemanly voice speaking.

"You've got a couple of tickets for sale?"

"Yes... I'll meet you out the front."

Over the gap between our seats, I tell Gemma, "I've got some buyers for the tickets, already."

I inspect the foyer for likely customers only to notice Gary Mooney and Lesley standing at the receptionist desk.

The purchasers are outside on the street, resplendent in their good fortune. The gentleman, white-haired and bearded, graciously pays the full amount for the tickets, exchanging $100 for the two of them. I am happy with this transaction and so are they.

Back in the foyer, I greet Gary and Lesley and ask them if they are travelling through. They explain that they are not, they have come from Newcastle for the concert alone and they are just leaving for a beer at the hotel.

I return to Gemma. "Well, that worked out well."

"Rick has phoned to tell me that they are on their way."

"Well, I won't be needing this on," I say, and make a show of turning off my mobile phone. But I doubt the act, thinking to myself, shouldn't I keep it on in case they need to contact me? It is merely courteous that this means of communication remains open for their benefit.

The commencement tone of the Nokia, followed by an automatic brightness, makes my covert action seem ludicrous. Then the option to configure the screen locked before I replace the phone in my pocket renders me puzzled.

There is a sign above the backstage door that invites us to partake in Chai and Cake. I join the other early-arrivals who have shown, and continue to show, an interest and an appetite for what is offered.

Inside the backroom, a small group of punters are sublimating their expectations for the gig while dutifully forming a queue to the kitchen's serving window. Conversations occur along the length of the patient line. Some queuers fiddle with their bags, purses or wallets while those who have reached the kitchen window make decisions about their orders. A receptive woman at the counter takes them into consideration and, along with the busy man next to her, pleasantly doles them out. The sweet stench of steamed pudding, slipped straight out of a can and doused with sauce ladled from a perfumed saucepan, creates a delicious air.

"And a chai tea, thanks."

With the warm cup in my left hand and a bowl of pudding in my right, I pass from the gathering crowd to the relative sanctuary of a stand-alone table. Here I consume the lovely drink and food with both an obedience and an indifference towards the time measured before the start of the show. After I grandly empty my hands of cup, bowl and spoon into a garbage bin, I re-enter the hall with the stride of someone famous.

Returning rather early yet to our front ranking row allows some time to observe the audience more. Past the civil woman taking her seat, a man in a shirt featuring Pink Floyd's iconic screamer from *The Wall* dances on the spot. Leaning in toward a seated friend, in animated conversation with her, the lively man embodies the movement of waves our audience is generating while we politely wait for something to happen. Due to his slogan, I turn to Gemma sitting next to Natasha and conspire tunefully for the second time today.

"Another brick in the wall."

We are close enough to the beginning now for me to close my phone down for sure.

I originally mistake the mingling figures to the side of the stage for members of the Tex, Don, and Charlie band, as they appear to occupy that marginal area with purposeful statures. However, when the two, noticeably younger, men set foot on the broad platform of the stage they attend only to the microphones placed at the front of the arch. The first has a long coat adding to his dangling locks, while the second, bearded and short-haired, is dressed in shirt sleeves. Together, they embark on a delightful dual guitar playing and vocal harmonising song-making evocative of laid-back sixties America. Our audience loves them.

"We are The Ahern Brothers," announces the longer of the two men, and someone's son. Then he necessarily corrects, because both have different surnames, "We are brothers in music."

Our audience gives a sigh.

Their second song continues in that tone of mutual respect. Once the tempo ceases, I turn to Gemma and share a brimful look.

A long-winded and good-natured introduction follows. The next song is a ballad written in homage to the stalwart companionship offered by the quieter performer's loyal girl-friend and later wife.

The Ahern Brothers' mutual description of awe at seeing a Giant Redwood forest segues to a song the artists say was inspired by a hardy wild tomcat they saw eking out a living in the forest's understorey. Its folky narration stimulates a memory of an adolescent romp I took into a clearing in Vermont in 1972. On a family road-trip across the northern States, a lone bushwalk resulted in my running naked from a stand of trees across a grassy field to a clump of fallen trunks. Bare and beautiful in my liberation, I had looked around to discover Dad looking on from the other side of the clearing. And later in the camp, with both our strolls having returned to Mum, Rick and Gemma, I remember, within the space claimed by the tent-trailer, the confidential awareness shared with Dad.

Rick and Kerry are found in the break after The Ahern Brothers have given thanks and left the stage.

Father and daughter are standing together by a fire door. Each says they have enjoyed the supporting act from their angle halfway up the gentle slope. Rick, beside Kerry, has regathered his composure. Kerry is an illustration of the trouble she went to in getting ready. Her dark hair falls, neatly brushed, down either side of her pictorially made-up face. There is a certain vogue in Kerry's choice of clothes that does not quite match the audience this evening. She is perhaps more suited to an eighties' dance floor where contemporary country plays alongside power ballads. But clothes do not *maketh* the woman, after all.

Brother and niece both express readiness to relocate to the seats we have saved for them.

Thirst, with an accompanying quiet desperation, has intruded on my consciousness. An internal consultation concluding that water must sensibly be obtained, sends me back to the chai and cake counter.

"Can I have a drink of water, please?"

She provides this from a cup filled over the kitchen sink.

"Thanks." I say, meaning it.

I stand theatrically apart, and against an unprovable continuum of social reality and time passing raise the cup to my lips in portioned sips, making a final, bigger swallow.

Conditioned by such a portion of hydrating fluid, I return to my seat and sit upright like a pregnant woman.

In front of us, a drummer enters to squat at his kit, a double bassist takes his partner for the next dance, and a steel guitarist mounts his saddle. Soon after, Charlie, Tex, then Don wander on. Don makes a claim on the keys, Tex on the central microphone and a secondary guitar, and Charlie on his chair and lap steel. They get stuck straight in, cruising into their trademark dark country forms like old hands.

Don Walker sits a bit menacingly, fingering notes under an icing of stone-white grey hair, leaning over a small pot belly.

The once edgy, lean sexiness of Tex Perkins is now embellished by a three-meals-a-day broadness and reminds me of Hubert Raymond who used to live across the street. He would let me in at all hours, his children sleeping down the hall. Hubert is since sadly deceased but the moniker 'larger than life' still applies.

Charlie Owen, off to one side, maintains a meaningful interaction on strings and chair.

The three lead us through their repertoire of sad but true, old and new songs about how pathetic we are, all delivered from a trundling momentum of coming down.

Tex, with his wallowing yet dignified lower range, grabs our attention as he tells the story of an expeditionary man who takes his wife to a promised land that turns out a tropical hell, only to address her years later in a song from where he lives alone in falling snow.

'Plan B' lives up to reputation. The doleful ballad, about a middle-aged man getting drunk and using porn, means more to me when I understand his lonely urge to substitute the longed-for ways of an ex-lover with dears found in the stream.

Don turns from his keyboard in the direction of Tex and begins wiggling his fingers as if they are communicating aerials. Tex responds with mock seriousness directing correlating signals toward the prominent forehead of Don. We are witnessing a native telepathic tuning mandatory for the performance of their impending duet. I can only describe the resulting aural effect of intertwined adamant whines and robust groans as like the noise a bike chain makes running through a derailleur.

Tough leather boots kick-start the group into a rollicking version of the dangerously mad 'Dead Dog Boogie'.

Time slows and allows the majesty of his lower range to endear us all to the Tex Perkins call.

I approach Gary and Lesley stationed at the end of their row. Sitting there, they appear entrenched in a longer imbibition, as if beached in the wake of the passed tide.

I ask them what they thought of the show. Then add, "I really liked that song about the man taking his wife to the tropics and him ending up in a snowy place."

Without speaking, they concur.

Their telling that they are camping in the showground beckons me to remember, "I camped there once... during the Global Carnival... it teemed down rain and the place was flooded... it's best not to camp at the base of the hill."

I wonder whether this camping together business means they are a couple. Self-conscious, Gary seems to entertain the same question.

"I'm here to celebrate my 60th birthday with my family."

"I would have thought 50th," says Lesley, giving a hug that's merely a tired expression of goodwill. "Did you have a cake?"

"Yes, we've had cake, lots of cake... but what I really want is a decent meal... I feel shitty."

"We had one at the pub."

Gemma arrives by my side. "This is my sister, Gemma."

We all agree that the show was grand. Around us chairs are getting stacked by gracious hands.

"No doubt I'll see you around the traps."

Lesley believes so. Gary seems to harbour some doubt.

Into the cool night air! The three of us have used the now opened fire door. Natasha and Gemma, with me in tow, make our way to the car parked down the back end of the building. Rick and Kerry have already left by the front door, in order to smoke cigarettes outside. My last sighting tonight of the habit-sharing father and daughter. Our royal departure by the side door has furnished me with a sovereign excuse to miss the merchandising stall in the foyer. The concert was enough!

From the backseat of our travelling car, I give a questionable account to Natasha and Gem of one of the band members who played so well. "He used to play in a band called The Shower Scene from Psycho... His father was the Costigan from The Costigan Report."

Gemma steers us onwards, back to Aunt Elizabeth's. Natasha sits dreamily, in anticipation of motoring on in Gemma's car to meet her resurgent ex-boyfriend down at The Jetty. And then she'll continue to her well-known ex-boyfriend's friend's house-warming party.

I am an empty vessel who requires some soul food and a place to eat. Upon entering Aunt Elizabeth's abode, thoughts of toast and Vegemite, or toast and peanut butter, settle on my tongue. An investigation of her pantry surprises me. A container of fresh, oily peanut butter stands on the shelf.

Two browned slices rise from the handsome toaster. Yet I doubt. Could the lid on the peanut butter container have been loose on its thread? Could this tardiness also mean the food is shelved beyond its use-by-date?

The good fortune of an appetite appeased, discovered here in the 12th hour of my 60th year, is scandalised by over-thinking, yet I permit my inspector to peruse the gift horse in its mouth. His goal is a tell-tale printed date, either on the lid or on the label.

When it comes time to sit in a corner, to eat the spreads on toasts, to drink the cup of tea, a look of agreement on my face does not meet my sister's late-eyed notice.

"Good night brother."

A sea of dolls occupies the narrow bedroom. A portrait of Uncle Gavin invites his ghost into the room. He is welcome, after all, this was his house too. On the wall, pastel paintings break in a row. Over a single bed.